1977-1948

851.4

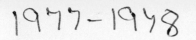
DATE DUE

DEC 1 5 1978			

Waters, John F.
    The Sea farmers

DEMCO

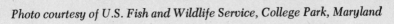

The Sea Farmers

Other books by JOHN F. WATERS:

Hastings House
MARINE ANIMAL COLLECTORS

Holiday House
SALTWATER AQUARIUMS

Dodd, Mead
WHAT DOES AN OCEANOGRAPHER DO?

Harvey House
SALTMARSHES AND SHIFTING DUNES

THE
SEA FARMERS

by JOHN F. WATERS

Illustrated with photographs

HASTINGS HOUSE, PUBLISHERS

New York

Second Printing, December 1971

Published simultaneously in Canada by
Saunders, of Toronto, Ltd., Don Mills, Ontario

ISBN: 8038-6690-9

Library of Congress Catalog Card Number: 71-98059
Printed in the United States of America

CONTENTS

ACKNOWLEDGMENTS

I am grateful to the following persons and institutions for their wonderful help in the preparation of THE SEA FARMERS:

Robert M. Ingle, Director of Research, Florida Board of Conservation; Stuart A. Campbell, Alpine Geophysical Associates; Iola I. Berg, Washington State Fisheries; Paul R. Ehrlich, Department of Biological Sciences, Stanford University; W. M. Rees, Marine Colloids, Inc.; William N. Shaw, U.S. Bureau of Commercial Fisheries, Oxford, Md.; F. W. Sieling, Department of Chesapeake Bay Affairs, U.S. Bureau of Commercial Fisheries, Oxford, Md.; James E. Hanks, Laboratory Director, Bureau of Commercial Fisheries, Milford, Conn.; Division of Fish and Game, Honolulu, Hawaii; C. P. Idyll, Chairman, Division of Fishery Sciences, Institute of Marine Sciences, Miami; Robert L. Dow, Marine Research Director, Department of Sea and Shore Fisheries, Augusta, Me.; Walter F. Godwin, Marine Biologist, Marine Fisheries Division of State Game & Fish Commission, Brunswick, Ga.; Edwin B. May, Biologist, State of Alabama Department of Conservation, Dauphin Island; Maximo J. Cerame-Vivas, Director, Department of Marine Sciences, University of Puerto Rico; G. Robert Lunz, Director, Bears Bluff Laboratories, Wadmalaw Island, South Carolina; Theodore P. Ritchie, Shellfisheries Biologist, University of Delaware, Lewes;

Austin R. Magill, Federal Aid Coordinator, Fish Commission State of Oregon, Portland; A. Russell Ceurvels, Marine Biologist, Department of Natural Resources, Division of Marine Fisheries, Boston; Paul Bauerfield and Robert R. Kifer, Animal Nutrition Unit, Bureau of Commercial Fisheries Technological Laboratory, College Park, Md.; E. W. Shell, Associate Professor of Fisheries, Auburn University, Auburn, Ala.; John L. Taylor, Fishery Biologist, Bureau of Commercial Fisheries Biological Laboratory, St. Petersburg Beach, Fla.; H. Arnold Carr, Shellfish Biologist, Shellfish Extension, Department of Marine Fisheries of the Commonwealth of Massachusetts, Sandwich; Chris H. Riley, Director, Division of Shell Fisheries of State of New Jersey Department of Conservation and Economic Development, Trenton.

Also J. G. Broom, Louisiana Wild Life and Fisheries Commission, Marine Laboratory, Grand Terre Island; Leon A. Verhoeven, Executive Director, Pacific Marine Fisheries Commission, Portland, Oregon; Charles M. Bearden, Bears Bluff Laboratories, Wadmalaw Island, South Carolina; Gordon Gunter, Gulf Coast Research Laboratory, Ocean Springs, Miss.; Thomas D. McIlwain, Project Leader Striped Bass in Miss., Gulf Coast Research Laboratory, Ocean Springs; James Lewis, St. Petersburg Times, St. Petersburg, Fla.; Kenneth D. Woodburn, Florida Board of Conservation Marine Laboratory, St. Petersburg; Seton H. Thompson, Director, Bureau of Commercial Fisheries, St. Petersburg Beach, Fla.; Milton T. Hickman, Commissioner, Marine Resources Commission, Newport News, Va.; Robert E. Stevens, Assistant Leader of the North Carolina Cooperative Fishery Unit, Bureau of Commercial Fisheries, Raleigh; Donald M. Harriman, Marine Fisheries Extension Agent, Department of Sea and Shore Fisheries, Augusta, Me.; Dan Regan, Division of Fish Hatcheries, Bureau of Sport Fisheries and Wildlife, Atlanta, Ga.; C. S. Kabel, Associate Marine Biologist, Marine Resources Branch, Department of Fish and Game of the State of California, Sacramento; W. A. Dahlstrom, Associate Marine Biologist, Marine Resources Operations Laboratory, Department of Fish and Game of the State of California, Sacramento; James B. Engle, Chief, Bureau of Commercial

Fisheries, Biological Laboratory, Oxford, Md.; Davidson A. Neal, Marine Biological Laboratory, Louisiana Wild Life and Fisheries Commission, Grand Isle; William C. Ayer, Marine Biologist, State of New Hampshire Fish and Game Department, Concord; Robert E. Schroeder, Executive Vice President, Mariculture, Ltd., Grand Cayman Island, B.W.I.; John Ryther and K. O. Emery of the Woods Hole Oceanographic Institution, Woods Hole, Mass.; Robert Edwards, Bureau of Commercial Fisheries, Woods Hole; John H. Finucane, Fishery Biologist, Bureau of Commercial Fisheries, St. Petersburg Beach, Fla.; and John J. Powell, Chemist, Bureau of Commercial Fisheries, College Park, Md.

A fish trap, strategically placed, will bring up a multitude of fish. *Courtesy of Miami Seaquarium*

1

The Sea: A Source of Life

The sea is a life source. The ocean, like the land, is a great producer of plants and animals that can be turned into food for man. Energy from the sun brings about a series of changes in the sea similar to the life cycle of animals on land. Just as green plants growing in the earth make proteins, carbohydrates and minerals that provide man's food so, in the sea, a similar process takes place. Knowing this, marine scientists are directing their attention to the oceans as a major source of food for man.

Billions of plants, so tiny they can be seen only with a microscope, float freely in the shallows of the sea. Each contains chlorophyll that allows it to combine chemicals with sunlight into a substance suitable for nourishment. These little plants, called phytoplankton, are made up of the algae and plant-animals that form the basic food of the sea. Tiny animals called zooplankton feed on the phytoplankton, while small fish feed on the zooplankton. Larger fish feed on the small ones.

Sifting down to the floor of the sea from the sunlit areas above are bits of animal and plant debris that star-

11

fish, crabs and other crustaceans feed upon before these particles decay. Sugars and starches from the decayed material are forced upward by underwater currents to the sunlit areas where the small plants, the phytoplankton, take them and combine them with sunlight, thereby changing themselves into food suitable for the animals of the sea. Thus the life cycle continues.

In recent years only about two percent of the whole world's total food supply has come from the ocean. This is mainly because man has not been able to accustom himself to ocean environment or to catch fish and other sea animals efficiently. Also, many people do not like to eat seafood except perhaps lobster or shrimp. Some believe, for example, that all fish smell and that squid are tasteless. They would not want to sit down to porpoise steak any more than they would think of eating puppy dog fritters.

If there is to be a mounting food shortage, as many scientists predict, would it not be better to farm more land? It is easier and cheaper to work on land; there are higher cash profits, and according to figures in the U.S. Department of Agriculture the harvest per acre of land is greater than the overall ocean harvest has been. Nevertheless, many scientists look to the sea as a new source of food because there is not that much unused farmland remaining. For example, in the United States where there are 2.3 billion acres of land, almost half this space is being farmed already. The rest of the acreage is needed increasingly for houses, schools, industries, roads, recreational areas and so on.

Some marine scientists say that there is enough potential food in the oceans to feed the world, no matter how large the population becomes. They believe that someday sea harvesting will be done with super instruments such as vacuums that can suck up and deposit entire schools of fish in the holds of huge ships; that men will train porpoises to herd fish much as dogs herd sheep; and that someday man will be eating burgers made of plankton that will be cheaper and tastier than the ones we eat today. Other scientists are not so optimistic, and say that the oceans will only be able to furnish sufficient animal protein to sustain a human population of ten billion, a population figure that is not too far in the future, if our present birthrate continues unchanged.

Two senior scientists, K. O. Emery and Columbus Iselin, from the Woods Hole Oceanographic Institution on Cape Cod in Massachusetts, feel that any substantial progress in harvesting food from the sea will come about only after a major change in men's attitudes. They have compiled studies showing that in 1964 100,000 tons of plants were gathered in a wild state from the ocean as compared with two million tons from land.* Plants actually grown in the ocean were practically nil compared to 230 million tons farmed or grown on land. Animals hunted in the ocean represented 1.6 million tons, compared to a little less, 1.3 million tons on land. There were 100,000 tons of animals farmed by man in the oceans and 85 million tons on land. These figures show that far more good is still taken from the sea by the primitive methods of hunting and gathering than by the more advanced farming methods used on land.

There is, however, a growing movement in the United States toward farming the seas. The public taste for lobsters, shrimp and other special seafoods has increased. For example, in the past 25 years the demand for shrimp has doubled. Also, through medical research we are becoming aware of the nutritional value of seafood. Since it contains unsaturated oils, greater consumption of seafood

*Science, Sept. 15, 1967, Vol, 157

will reduce the saturated fat intake that leads to high blood cholesterol, one of the contributing factors in heart disease.

Some marine scientists predict that the demand for seafood in the United States will continue to increase in the next few years, and this should raise the present market price. It has been proved that farm-raised oysters, shrimp, fish, and other forms of sea life are of better quality than those caught or taken from public grounds. Sea farming might also help to solve the problem of deciding what areas belong to what nations and who is to police these areas once they are designated. There have always been complications in determining territorial rights along the shorelines. There have also been problems about controlling the catch. To date, fishing control, as proved by the continued overfishing of whales, has not been successful. An international commission now sets a limit on the catch of whales, but it may already be too late for the blue whales and others whose numbers are dangerously low. There is still no international police force to see that nations and their fleets abide by the rules. By farming seafood, each nation could assure itself of a certain supply of a species, regardless of what other countries do.

In the United States farming of the sea is a relatively new method of taking food from the ocean and not too popular as yet, at least compared to the interest and progress shown by other countries. Most foreign fishermen hunt the sea for food. Our fishermen demand profit.

2

Feeding the Millions

In a speech before the Commonwealth Club of California in 1967, Dr. Paul R. Ehrlich of the Department of Biological Sciences of Stanford University said that the idea of feeding millions of people with food from the sea is a pipe dream. He maintained that the population of the world will grow to such a size that no kind of technological development will make it possible to feed these millions, either from the sea or from any other source on this planet. In a similar vein a British physicist, J. H. Fremlin, has put a theoretical limit on the population of this world. It is his belief that when there are one billion billion people on the earth the heat converted from the energy of all these people will prevent additional life from developing. When this time comes about 120 persons will inhabit each square yard of the earth's surface. They will all be housed in a building two thousand stories high that will cover the entire surface of the earth, land and sea alike. Each person will have three or four yards of floor space to call his own and, because of the heat energy, travel will be limited to a few hundred yards. One nice feature is that each person could select his friends from the millions living in the same apartment building. It is reassuring to be told that all this is expected to come only nine hundred years from now.

Fremlin's theory may or may not come true, but it does seem likely that man will have tremendous difficulty feeding himself when the population is double what it is today. If we believe that the hope of feeding such numbers is a pipe dream then many marine scientists are wasting their precious time. It might be better for them to forget these theories about the future and concentrate on what is happening now. However, it was not too long ago that man thought it impossible to fly in the sky, send rockets into space, land on the moon, or dive more than seven miles down to the bottom of the sea. In fact, only about five hundred years ago men believed there was no way to sail around the world because ships would surely fall off the edge.

No one can really know what is going to happen a thousand years from now. They can only speculate. The past has shown us that man often outdoes even his fondest hopes with his inventions and ingenuity. With this in mind, man can look forward hopefully to devising a method of taking enough food from the sea or air, or from the sun's energy to support a population of many billions.

For a start, marine scientists have been working on a method of processing fish flour, known as marine protein concentrate or MPC. It has no aroma and becomes invisible when added to other foods, but it still contains a high percentage of the vitamins, proteins and minerals needed to sustain a healthy life. There is the problem that just the mention of fish flour sends some people to the window for fresh air. But that need not be the case. Other foods have been processed into various forms: wheat is ground into flour; corn made into cereal; even milk and

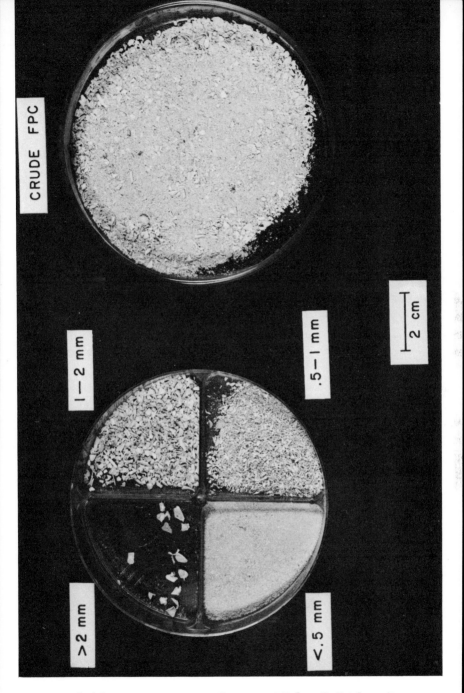

Crude fish protein concentrate. *Courtesy of Robert K. Brigham, Bureau of Commercial Fisheries, U.S. Fish and Wildlife Service*

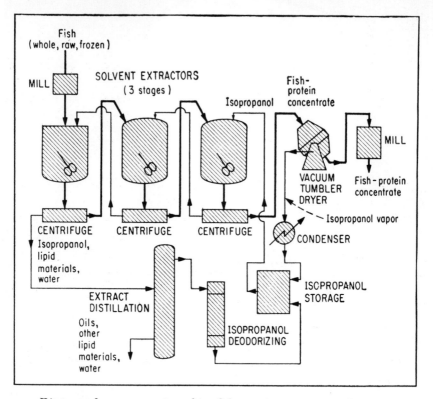

Diagram of one process in making fish protein concentrate. *Courtesy of Bureau of Commercial Fisheries, College Park. Md.*

eggs, when dried, have many uses. This kind of idea is not new. The Romans had something called liquamen. In the late 1800's there were fish flour biscuits. Later, other kinds of dried and ground fish were processed for food.

Scientists feels it is now time to get a world-wide production system started for MPC. They say there are enough fish in the ocean to make this possible. It is estimated by some marine scientists that only ten percent of the ocean's annual supply of fish is presently being harvested by man. Fishermen do not yet have the manpower or equipment to bring in large catches and even they readily admit that half their potential haul is left at sea.

Extraction vessels used in processing fish protein concentrate. *Courtesy of Bureau of Commercial Fisheries, College Park, Md.*

It has been pleaded by many people that MPC can be the answer right now to the hunger of millions throughout the world, and that too little is being done to relieve present day malnutrition. Even so at one of the prime whaling ports of the previous century, New Bedford, Mass., the first marine protein concentration plant in the United States was dedicated in April of 1968. This plant uses the VioBin process, a method of removing the fat from the tissues of fish at the same time dehydration is taking place. Using this and other methods, it is now possible to produce MPC economically and in enough quantity to supply present market demands. One hun-

dred thousand pounds of fish are processed daily to produce twenty tons of MPC that has not been deodorized
and is used for feeding animals. This would amount to
sixteen tons of deodorized MPC fit for human consumption.

At the New Bedford plant, a type of hake is fed into
a closed processing system that begins by grinding up the
whole fish in a feed mill. The resulting mash then goes
through a long, complicated system of tanks, pipes, extrac-
tors, vats, filters, dryers and grinders before it is finally
sifted through a screen. Then the flour is ready for animal
food. Additional purifying equipment is used to upgrade
the product for human consumption. It is important to
note that the nutrient content of fish meal varies according to the fish and the process used. Therefore, throughout the world, there is a marked difference in fish-meal
quality and projects are under way to set universal
standards.

In various parts of the world, human grade MPC has
been used as a substitute for milk in feeding babies, and
has also been mixed with corn, wheat, rice, soups, tor-
tillas, soybean flour, breads and other foods.

Since land animals are also needed to help feed a
hungry world, it was certainly a boon to discover that
MPC worked as an animal food. Chickens, turkeys, small
pigs, calves, cows, horses, dogs, and cats are fed the concentrate. Even fish kept in captivity are fed the flour. It is
fine for the growth of young animals, for fattening stock,
or for enriching an animal's fur. It can be used as a special rich food for zoo animals, for improving pet foods, or
for bringing sick or injured animals back to health.

Most important, MPC is a world feeder. This means
it can be used in any country at any time because it is an
odorless and tasteless powder. It is not banned by a par-
ticular religion, prejudice or custom. However there are

still more hazards to its consumption. For example, there is a remote possibility that whole schools of fish can become poisoned while in the ocean. The poison may not kill the fish but will accumulate in their tissues. If, by chance, the contaminated school is caught and processed there is a danger of the poison — such as the kind that leaks from sunken shipwrecks — being transmitted. As yet there is no certainty as to what causes such contamination, although metals from the wrecked ships are among the suspected causes. Another hazard is that the muscles of some fish contain large quantities of free histidine that can change to histamine under bad storage conditions, causing allergic reactions or poisoning when eaten. Not enough is known about this complication as yet, but it can be seen that constant study and many precautions in the processing methods must be continued.

Fish oils are another source of food and are directly related to fish flour since they are a by-product of the fish-meal processing method. The oils are used outside the United States mainly for margarine, shortening and cooking fats and are used within the United States as industrial oils that are valuable in greases, paper sizing, lubricants, buffing agents, textile dyes and inks. These oils are much lower in price than the oil from peanuts, sunflowers, cottonseed or soybeans. They also contain various amounts of vitamins A and D, found in the liver of the fish, as well as a quantity of vitamin E, necessary in the diets of animals to prevent certain diseases. Fish oils fed to chickens increase egg production. They can be fed to pigs, cattle and goats and when proper doses are given the animals grow fatter, the cow's milk increases, the animals' health improves and they possess high levels of energy.

Marine scientists, conscious of the need for more food from the sea, have been thinking of possible ways for enlarging the catch of fish. Jacques-Yves Cousteau, a French undersea explorer who has taken thousands of dives, has observed that fish naturally tend to use sunken ships as living quarters. He proposes that a concrete building be constructed for each species with several floors and pipes used to transport the necessary nutrients to the fish. Dr. Joseph H. Slavin and Dr. John D. Kaylor of the Bureau of Commercial Fisheries in Gloucester, Massachusetts believe that the use of cobalt 60, a radioactive isotope that emits invisible electromagnetic rays, should be used to kill bacteria found in fish that have been caught. With the elimination of these bacteria, fish could be transported greater distances in a much fresher condition.

Some scientists have found that fish react to what they hear, see, smell and feel. Research has shown that fish line up facing the positive pole when put into an electric field. After lining up they tend to drift toward the pole and continue to do so as long as the electricity is applied. In actual experiments, when the fish came near the positive pole, they were stunned and were easily caught by scooping them out of the water. So far this method has been successful in fresh water, but has not proved efficient in the sea because the conductivity of salt water requires the use of more electric current.

Some fishing vessels already have various forms of new equipment. The Russians have been catching fish called kilka, which swim near the mouth of a tube where powerful suction draws them out of the water onto the deck of the fishing vessel.

The use of spacecraft in improving the catch is being explored and, experiments to date show that it may become effective. Fish oils can be detected on the surface of the ocean by the use of infrared instruments on the spacecraft. The presence of these fish oils usually means that fish are feeding nearby in schools. It can also be determined from a spacecraft if this oil is fresh and the information can then be relayed to land-based tracking stations. They in turn send this news to the captains of fishing vessels in the area.

Iodine vapors also can be spotted from space. The marine animals and plants that fish feed on give off 100,000 times as much iodine as plain sea water. By detecting this iodine concentrate, the spacecraft can locate a fish-feeding area and fishing boat captains can be told of the location.

Some of these ideas will work; others may not. But marine scientists will surely find ways of improving the catch and thus bringing more fish and more food to more people. How many will be fed, only time will tell.

Young salmon fry ready for migration to salt water. *Courtesy of Washington State Department of Fisheries*

3

The Fish Farmers

The United States Department of Interior's report on fish kills in rivers and streams in 1966 showed that nine million fish were destroyed by pollution in that year alone. And this is not the entire total since many kills go unobserved or unreported. In one lake in Florida the wastes from a citrus-processing plant caused overmultiplication of algae and the end result was that as the tiny plants decayed the bacteria used up all the available oxygen in the lake. Over one million fish died, actually from drowning since they were unable to get needed oxygen from the water. An additional million fish were destroyed in a river in Pennsylvania when a rainstorm washed acid deposits from a mine into the river.

Our country's estuaries, the arms or inlets where rivers meet the sea, are a special problem. Something is being done now to start cleaning up the pollution, but factories are still pouring wastes and chemicals into rivers, and these work their way down into the shallow areas of the sea where tiny fish and other small marine creatures live. Often these wastes kill baby fish or destroy the food

25

they need, leaving little or nothing alive. Yet it is in clean estuarine waters that the fish farmer can operate best. He can dig a pond-farm out of the marshes of the estuary and deliver more pounds of protein per acre than in the rich fishing grounds off the coasts. Close control over the animals can be maintained. The amount of salt in the water can be checked, better feed provided and diseases watched. Most important top quality fish eggs can be used and hatched successfully.

Throughout the world just a few hundred thousand acres of estuaries are used in pond culture for fish farming. These estuaries and marshes are the storage ground for the valuable nutrients required by various marine animals. These beds of grass, mud and sand help produce many fish and shellfish, and serve as a nursery for hundreds of species of animals in their first few months of life. Still, there is not much fish farming in the United States. What little is being done is mostly of an experimental nature. The men who work as researchers in this area are concentrating on a broad, two-point program: cleaning up the pollution, and increasing the catch by preventing overfishing and maintaining the numbers of existing fish.

One typical fish farm is located in Ardote, Scotland. Two dams have been built making a sea loch, and the fry, or small fish, of the sole family are kept behind them. Warm water from a nuclear power station is used to rear the fish during the cold winter months, as fish grow little during the winter unless placed in warm water.

Buildings containing salt water trays hold the fish eggs, which remain in these rearing tanks until shortly after hatching. The baby fish are fed brine shrimp, an excellent food. At first, the small fish eat ten brine shrimp a day but in three months their need increases to more than 200 per day. In 1965 the first batch of plaice, a flat bottom fish, was transferred to the loch but shore crabs attacked them and heavy rains diluted the water, causing widespread losses. Problems like this have since been solved and to-day fish are growing rapidly in this farm that has a capacity for raising one million fish.

Studies have also produced results in the United States. In 1966 it was announced that Pacific sardines and mackerel had been raised from eggs to an advanced juvenile state at the Bureau of Commercial Fisheries California Current Resources Laboratory at La Jolla. The mackerel reached a length of ten inches, about half the adult size, and the sardines grew to four inches or about one-third the adult size. To date, 15 species of marine fish have been raised from the egg stage in this experimental aquarium by Dr. George O. Schumann.

An important part of this experiment was the feeding — making sure the fish received the proper food at the right time. Young fish were fed bits of microscopic animals and plants (plankton) and as they increased in size, more plankton, and then brine shrimp. Large amounts of food plus warm water enabled some of the small fish to double their size in two weeks. The experiments were part of a study of the habits and life history of mackerel and sardines undertaken to preserve the mackerel market and to try to make the sardine fisheries as productive again as they were in the middle 1940's.

An attempt has been made to raise pompano, an excellent food fish, in the laboratory at the United States Bureau of Commercial Fisheries at St. Petersburg, Florida. John H. Finucane, a bureau biologist, heads the fish farm project. The farm consists of a fenced-off lagoon that allows the fish to swim about in six acres of freedom. The fence keeps out unwanted species of fish and possible predators while allowing tidal circulation and constant exchange of water. These fish may prove difficult to raise

Measuring and weighing fish to determine growth rate in pompano pond at Fort De Soto Park, Florida. *Courtesy of Bureau of Commercial Fisheries, St. Petersburg Beach, Florida*

in large numbers as they have no teeth and are unable, while young, to attack and eat free-swimming marine animals. Studies have shown that pompano in captivity prefer sand fleas, and coquina, a tiny and beautiful member of the clam family, but it is hard to collect enough of this food to nourish large stocks of pompano. Trash fish and fish discarded by shrimpers have been used successfully as feed during the first two months of growth. So have frozen adult brine shrimp, fish fillets, and ground frozen shrimp. During advanced growth stages, ground shrimp heads and fish meal have proved satisfactory as food. However, if an artificial food can be found, the farming of pompano will become easier.

Variances in temperature and salinity do not harm these fish as much as they can harm other species. The limits are not known exactly, but water temperatures below 50° Fahrenheit are injurious and can wipe out the whole school. Although pompano are being raised on farms from eggs, it is still a question whether this can become commercially profitable. Large schools of young fish, a half to one inch in length, are easily netted off the north Florida coast between April and November. One farm; a two and a half acre pond, is presently raising pompano netted while young to sell commercially when they are grown. This may become a well-paying business practice since there is already a good market demand for pompano.

Seining pompano to check on mortality at pompano pond. *Courtesy of Commercial Fisheries, St. Petersburg Beach, Florida*

Mullet are farmed easily but do not bring a prime price on the market. Because they feed on algae and the small plants and animals found in mud, they do not have to be given food, as do the pompano. Changes of sea water will bring in crustaceans and other forms of food. The mullet can stand a high salt content and high water temperatures but do not fare well in lower temperatures. The only part of the United States where mullet are farmed to any degree is in the Hawaiian islands, which used to be a popular area for fish farming. This business has dropped off considerably in the past 70 years. The mullet, called *ama ama* by the Hawaiians, was the primary fish raised out of about thirteen species farmed before 1900. Salt water or brackish ponds were blocked off at the entrance to the bay with piles of lava rock, which acted as strainers allowing water to trickle through while keeping the fish in. The fish-farm owners were kings or chiefs of the island and the workers were the commoners of that time. After the turn of the century, rice culture developed into a more important business and many of the pond-farms became overgrown. Other ponds suffered because their location stood in the way of the new tourist industry. One was at the now famous Waikiki Beach and another major pond was filled in for real-estate development. In 1900 approximately 485,000 pounds of fish were harvested yet in 1960 the figure had dropped to only 33,000 pounds.

Dr. Lauren R. Donaldson, professor of fisheries at the University of Washington in Seattle, has been working with Chinook salmon. In 1949 a salmon run was started so that after the fertilized eggs had brooded the tiny fish could be released into a pond that eventually led out to salty Puget Sound. At that time it was not known if artificially reared salmon would find their way back to their native ponds every four years as do salmon born in natural surroundings. To the surprise of many, the first

Spawning salmon on upstream migration. *Courtesy of Washington State Departmentof Fisheries*

few fish came back to their pond three years later, in 1952. From those that returned, Dr. Donaldson and his team began selecting the females and biggest males for breeding purposes. Over the years, as more fish returned, the researchers kept the best fish for breeding: those that had a better color, better shape, bigger size, and the best health.

Now, more than 20 seasons have elapsed since the first fish were bred. Over half of these farm-bred fish return in three years, instead of the usual four. The weight of most returnees is twelve pounds — a little above average — and they are over thirty inches in length. But the greatest surprise of this experiment was the discovery that

Feeding dry pellet feed to young salmon. *Courtesy of Washington State Department of Fisheries*

these fish have an ability to survive in the ocean at a rate ten to 30 times greater than the naturally bred salmon.

One interesting feature of this study is the fact that these fish are not pampered, but are kept in what might be called dirty water. These salmon farmers are attempting to breed a super fish, one that can survive pollution. The water of their farm is kept at natural temperatures to prepare the fish for the rigors of ocean living, as well as fresh water lakes, rivers and streams. The young salmon eat a food prepared from whole hake. This treatment has proven to be best for developing the quality of the fish as well as its size and ability to survive the hardships at sea. First the hake is ground up, then enzymes within the hake partially digest it, while the bacteria growth is slowed down through temperature and acidity controls. Wheat germ and rice hulls, rich in vitamin B, are added. The small salmon digest this food more easily than MPC and in six months grow to twice the size of salmon fed on other diets.

In 1967 Dr. E. Wayne Shell and John R. Kelley, Jr. from Auburn University in Alabama conducted a year's research on the possibility of rearing striped bass in the Mobile Bay area surrounding estuaries. About 10,000 striped bass fry were obtained from a hatchery and placed in gallon hatching jars. The fish were fed every hour for 168 hours on whole egg solids mixed with water and blended with yeast plus an artificial food designed for salmon. When the fry reached a length of one to one and a half inches they were placed in three ponds with about 2,000 small bass in each pond. They were fed trout chow that was floated on the top of the water. It is interesting to note that they stopped feeding when the water had grown cloudy from rains, yet as soon as the water cleared they began feeding again. Since different types and amounts of food were used in each of the three ponds the results varied, but all facts obtained were promising. It was learned that striped bass can be grown to six or more inches in about three months on pelleted feed alone, and that the amount of money and time required by the farmer of bass leaves him room to make a profit. It was also estimated that 1,000 to 2,000 pounds of bass could be raised per acre, with few dying off. Results of the experiment indicate that striped bass may be raised economically without using natural food and probably at a lower cost than trout or salmon.

Another reason for promoting fish farming is to provide a recreation area for anglers. This could be done if a fish farmer stocked a pond with game fish, fed them until they were large enough to tempt the fisherman, then opened up for business. The proprietor would make his income by charging a fee for fishing in the area, or by charging by the pound for any fish caught. Money could also be collected in boat rentals, bait sales, or in operating a sandwich stand.

The United States has millions of sportsmen who really enjoy their fishing. For example, there is the story of the cruiser San Diego sunk off the coast of Long Island, New York, by a German submarine in 1918. The wreck served as a home for fishes and other marine life. It was not until 1955 that a charter-boat fishing captain accidentally found the wreck, tossed over his line, and brought

Typical salmon hatchery at Toutle River, Washington. *Courtesy of Washington State Department of Fisheries*

up a good sized specimen of fluke. He soon realized he had found a virtual undersea mine of fish. He kept his secret as long as he could but the good news eventually leaked out to the other fishermen. A salvage company finally bought the hull from the Navy and was about to raise it to sell the metal when the sports fishermen got up in arms against the firm, enlisted the help of New York Senator Kenneth B. Keating and the American Littoral Society, and convinced everyone that the salvage contract should be canceled, thereby saving the artificial fish reef.

Because of this and similar incidents marine scientists and others decided that artificial reefs might be a boon to fishermen as well as an aid to fish farming in the future. Since 1950 ocean scientists have been testing junk materials that might attract fish by loading them into barges and dropping them overboard at sites considered ideal for fish production. Items used included auto tires, stripped auto chassis, streetcars, ship hulls, broken culverts, pipes, rubble from old buildings, concrete blocks, and even fabricated fish "homes" of poured concrete. It has been found that better fishing resulted in most of these areas. For example, building rubble dropped off the New York coast improved fishing in that area, and six streetcars dumped off the California coast attracted sand bass and kelp bass by the thousands. In Hawaii several hundred junk cars used to form an artificial reef increased the fishing in that area from 36 pounds per acre to 1,500 pounds. So far the commercial fisherman has shown little interest in artificial reefs and continues the habit of searching for new grounds. But the day will arrive, as scientists now know, when new grounds will cease to exist.

Many people from different fields of study are needed to work together on the artificial reef project. One must know in advance the contour of the ocean bottom in a certain location in order to fasten the reef. Currents, storm action and effects of silt, should be studied by the physical oceanographer. The chemical oceanographer would watch and tabulate the effects of salt water, fish, and other marine life on the reef and how the materials affected the fish. The ocean engineer would work out the design of the reef, how it would be transported, and how it should be placed. Buoys should mark the reef properly. Biologists must find out if temperature, light, depth, food, and bottom surroundings in the location are suitable.

The University of South Florida has started a reef project covering about a hundred acres in the Gulf of Mexico in order to see how many pounds of fish per acre can be expected under such conditions. This may be the way fish farms eventually will be formed in the United States. Dr. William Taft, director of sponsored research at the University, believes that someday 27,000 square miles of evenly spaced reefs may dot the continental shelves, owned by various companies which will harvest fish from their own reefs. These reefs will probably be constructed of concrete or other durable material. While it is sometimes convenient to use junk and streetcars, these materials last only about four years before crumbling away and needing replacement, making it an expensive operation since transportation costs are high.

Even if fishing reefs work, a new fight must begin against the pollution from offshore oil drilling rigs both off the U.S. coast and other countries along the continental shelf. Many scientists claim that these rigs drastically cut into the fish population although some oil men claim that fish gather near them. Also, when oil research ships set out to find oil and set off seismic blasting, fish are disturbed or even killed. Oil men say the kill is insignificant, but fishermen who have observed fish carcasses floating as far as the eye can see do not agree.

Because of such threats Representative Hastings

Four ¼ acre man made salt water ponds at Bureau of Commercial
Fisheries biological laboratory in Oxford, Md. *Courtesy of Robert
K. Brigham, Bureau of Commercial Fisheries, U.S. Fish and Wild-
life Service*

Keith of Massachusetts has suggested that a fish preserve
be set off the shores of Cape Cod. There would be no
licenses handed out to oil companies for exploration
within their boundaries. It would be much like the Federal Wilderness Preserves the United States Government
has already established in forests, plains and mountains
to keep these in their natural state. This is a program that
will certainly be given much thought as a possible aid in
the development of the future supply of fish.

Large lobster. *Courtesy of Robert K. Brigham, Bureau of Commercial Fisheries, U.S. Fish and Wildlife Service*

4

Raising Lobsters

Lobsters have always been a seaside New England treat but with the widespread use of the airplane, live lobsters are now shipped to every state in the Union. Today, lobsters wholesale for $1.00 a pound and, during the summer when the supply is short and the demand is heavy, the market price is $2.00 and may go higher. In short, more and more people want lobster to eat and the supply is too low to meet the demand.

Lobsters have been enjoyed for centuries. The Indians caught this marine animal and ate it in quantity long before they introduced it to the Pilgrims. Squaws used to plunge into the icy waters off Massachusetts and Maine to pluck lobsters barehanded. Early colonists mentioned their succulence in their records as have succeeding generations.

In spite of this long-time acquaintance with the lobster, marine scientists lack information about the creature — such as exactly how long it lives, how far it travels, what the size of its population might be, what it eats, the diseases that afflict it, or the best environment for it to live in. One thing is not a mystery however, and that is the fact that lobsters have hard shells and must molt or split out of their shells in order to grow. Breeding takes place during this molting period. Eggs develop inside the female but do not hatch until almost two years after the time of mating. During half of this period the eggs are carried inside the body and during the other half under the tail. A small lobster, weighing about two pounds, may hatch 30,000 baby lobsters but only about 30 of these little fry will live for as long as three weeks. This tremondous loss is mainly due to the fact that lobster fry are very, very tiny. They float to the top of the sea and are immediately attacked by fish from below and birds from above. Those that do survive molt rapidly at first, about four times in the first three-week period. After this the two front claws are usable and the babies are like adults in form, but are still only a half inch in length. At this age they stop floating and sink to the bottom, where they spend the remainder of their lives. They feed there but not as scavengers as people once thought. They eat fish, shellfish, and even their own kind if there is an opportunity, but they will not touch spoiled food.

Lobster fishing takes place off the east coast of the United States in waters ranging from inshore areas only a few feet deep to offshore waters of 1,500 feet or more. It is known that the best places to catch lobster are rocky environments, although they can be found almost anywhere. Small lobster boats that are fast and maneuverable allow the lobstermen to pull their pots quickly. These pots are set out in strings of 25, 50, or 100 or more. They are found and identified by means of a lobster buoy attached to a line from the lobster pot. Each buoy has the specific colors and markings of the lobsterman who owns the pot, which is usually made of wood and weighted down with bricks, although rubber and plastic-coated metal pots are now becoming popular. The pot has two compartments with funnelshaped nets leading inside that make it easy for a lobster to enter but difficult for it to leave. Bait, such as fish-heads or bags of dried, ground fish parts are tied inside the second compartment. The lobster crawls in, attracted by the smelly bait, and is trapped. This method of catching has been used for years, and new designs for lobster pots have failed to improve the catch.

On his daily rounds the lobsterman raises the pot to his boat with the help of a winch. Short lobsters and females are thrown back, since the law of most states protects these in order that the lobster population can grow.

Dragging is one method used for gathering the huge deep-water lobsters that grow much larger than their brothers near the shore. Fishing draggers set out nets and drag the bottom. It is not unusual to bring back lobsters weighing twenty-five pounds or more and the price per pound is usually much less. Contrary to belief, the meat is not tough but very tasty. The only problem is in finding a cooking utensil in the kitchen large enough to boil a creature three feet long.

The third procedure involves the use of lobster tankers. These are 170-foot vessels equipped with refrigerated tanks that can hold 100,000 pounds of lobster. A crew works in three shifts, hauling and tending 40,000 traps over a four week period. These ships are capable of servicing offshore lobster grounds where the seas are too rough for the conventional trawler and the distance too great for the inshore trap lobsterman.

The state of Maine is responsible for about 80% of the lobster catch along the east coast of the United States from Labrador to North Carolina. The greatest abundance of lobster is found in this area. Half the lobsters consumed in the United States are imported from Canada.

Lobsters are flown by jet from New England to Germany in fifteen hours or reach Los Angeles in time for lunch if shipped the same morning.

Many attempts have been made to raise lobsters along the Pacific coast. Before 1900 four different projects were carried out during which 104,000 larvae and more than 350 adult lobsters were planted off California. Adult lobsters were released off the Washington coast and some were even placed in Great Salt Lake in Utah. All the experiments failed. Again, between the years 1906 and 1917 almost 25,000 lobsters were transplanted. These also failed to survive and reproduce. In 1954 the same scheme was tried again off the coast of Prince Rupert in British Columbia. Two years after this release several lobsters were caught, further south one of which had migrated 20 miles. It is now known that lobsters can be transplanted if the water in their new area is not too warm and other conditions are just right. Exactly what these requirements are has not yet been determined.

During recent years the Maine coast catch of lobsters has increased only slightly even though the number of pots has risen from 500,000 to 800,000 in the last ten years. Maine lobstermen feel the waters have been overfished, causing this developing scarcity. But scientists think the scarcity is due to the change in water temperature. In colder water the lobster moves around less, eats less, and takes more time to grow to legal size. It is believed that a cycle of cool air that may last for twenty years is now lowering the temperature of the water. But if the diminished catch is due to overfishing in the northeast a legal limit could be imposed to help serve this sea animal. For example, there could be a limit on the number of licenses issued and the number of traps allowed for each fisherman. The season for hunting lobsters could be six months a year instead of all year as is presently the

Underwater apartment house for lobsters. *Courtesy of State of Maine: Department of Sea and Shore Fisheries*

case. Even now there are severe restrictions on the lobster catch: no females with eggs may be taken, no short lobsters less than three and ³⁄₁₆ of an inch from the eye socket to the end of the body shell may be kept, and anyone caught raiding another man's lobster pot is heavily fined.

Because of the danger of overfishing, marine scientists in Maine are working on a plan to farm lobsters by putting them in warm water ocean flats or apartment houses. Lobsters cannot be farmed like fish in ponds because of the long period it takes for them to reach full size (about five years) and because of their cannibalistic tendencies. Therefore, it is felt that lobsters should be helped to grow while in the ocean. What has been proposed is similar to an artificial reef for fish — a warm water apartment (warm in relation to present day cold Maine ocean water) that will use thermally polluted or heated water from a power plant located at Cousin's Island in Maine. Biologists believe that warmer water may help the lobster population to increase, and may also help to attract the type of food they need for survival.

Scuba divers and marine biologists have prepared the lobster farm from about a hundred concrete blocks, each having two or three holes. A site was selected that had the best flow and also appeared to be the most natural habitat for lobsters. These blocks were placed in the water off Spruce Point near Cousin's Island in two rows, each several layers tall. Scuba divers then gathered rock from the area and stacked it around the reef to give it a natural look so that incoming lobsters would not be disturbed by the appearance. The power plant has the capacity to discharge 130,000 gallons of 65° water per minute. When the farm is operating the water will be channeled to the reef and, it is hoped, will spur the growth of animals around it. Since warm water rises and cold water sinks to the bottom it was necessary to conduct water-flow tests earlier. Dyes were placed in the water near the intake of the power plant and then followed as they went through the plant system and discharged back into the harbor.

It will take some time to find out if the lobster farm will be successful. If it does succeed, then it will be refined. Plastic capsules will be added to offer protection from their enemies to the very young lobsters. Each capsule will have attached hoses to supply heated water.

Treated sewage may be sent in through hoses to see if it will attract the type of marine life the lobsters find tempting to eat.

Water temperatures off the coast of Maine used to be on a norm of about 49° but presently are averaging 45°, and may become cooler. If the warm water described above proves to be an aid to lobster development then it will be easy to use elsewhere, since there are many plants discharging heated water. If this day comes and other marine life is not adversely affected, then instead of cursing power plants as pollutants we may find that they have become useful aids to preserving valuable fisheries.

Spawning tanks at shrimp hatchery in Takamatsu, Japan. *Courtesy of C. P. Idyll*

5

Shrimp Farmers

When someone is called a shrimp he is usually smaller than most people his age. But one of the giants of the seafood industry, especially in the United States and Japan, is the real shrimp. Delicate in taste, it can be cooked in a variety of ways and is often eaten as a before-dinner appetizer.

Most shrimp are still brought to market by way of shrimp boats because shrimp farming has not taken hold to any great extent in the United States. Shrimp reach marketable size in about six to ten months, which would make raising them feasible as far as time is concerned but the price so far has not been high enough to attract many farmers.

One of the largest shrimp farms in the world has been established in Japan but only during the last few years has the farm made any money. It sells live shrimp to restaurants and hotels for a special dish called tempura, a form of fried shrimp. In the off-season market, prices reach a high of $5.00 a pound. In the United States about one-fourth of that price is common. That in itself explains why

Japan has shrimp farms and the United States has only a few.

The operation in Japan was started by Dr. Motosaku Fujinaga who raises shrimp from eggs. The females are usually purchased from commercial fishermen and then brought to the farm where they are put in small tanks to lay their eggs. The eggs average about 500,000 per shrimp, but some females carry over a million. After spawning, the females are removed from the small tanks to prevent them from eating their own eggs. Shrimp are cannibalistic.

The eggs are constantly being moved in circulating water kept in motion by air pumped in from the bottom. In half a day the eggs hatch into the first of many stages of growth that take place in the shrimp's life cycle. There can be as many as ten stages, depending on the species.

For a day and a half after hatching, the shrimp feed on an internal yolk sac. After 36 hours they must begin to search for food, but since they are poor hunters as babies they can only feed on something directly in front of them. The first experiments in feeding failed because the type of food used settled to the bottom where few of the baby shrimp were able to find it. The food used by Dr. Fujinaga today is a tiny diatom, a very small marine algae. It is grown in vats on the shrimp farm, scooped up and placed in the tanks with the small shrimp. The circulating water in the tank keeps the diatoms afloat where the shrimp can see them and feed easily. At a later stage of development the shrimp eat oyster eggs, brine shrimp, clam eggs or copepods.

Finally, the shrimp are moved outdoors to small ponds where they stay for ten to twenty days before being moved to larger ponds for maturing. When the shrimp have reached marketing size, they are cooled to slow down their metabolism or life processes so that they will require

Shrimp draining pond. *Courtesy of Louisiana Wild Life and Fisheries Commission, Marine Laboratory*

little oxygen in order to live. They are packed in chilled sawdust, which keeps them alive for two days in warm weather and four days in winter, on their way to the tempura restaurants.

It is recommended that new shrimp farms in the United States be set up in brackish water ponds. After adult shrimp have migrated to the open sea to spawn, the baby shrimp migrate or drift back to estuarine areas during their many growth stages. As the shrimp grow in these marshy locales anyway it is only necessary for the shrimp farmer to alter the environment enough to increase the poundage of shrimp per acre. This is done through proper feeding, since the shrimp are already well adapted to the temperature and salt changes in the brackish pond.

The species of shrimp to be cultivated are mainly of four types: white, pink, brown and Carribean brown. All of these are quite similar: about nine inches in length and with a life span of one or two years. There are also several species of large river shrimp that may be used in pond culture.

The site of the pond should be exposed to tidal action, so that the water is constantly exchanged. Salinity tests can be used to guarantee that the pond will have only a little less salt than that of the ocean. The bottom should be a mixture of sand and clay. A marsh, lagoon or swamp can be dug out and a dike erected with a sluice gate. Connected to the main pond there will be other dikes and gates leading to the rearing ponds and nursery ponds. The gates are needed to change the water, and adjustable boards in the gates control the tidal flow and water level. The large pond should be dug so that it slopes toward the main gate, thus allowing it to be drained at low tide after the removal of all drawboards. A pond system of this type could cover about twenty-five acres. Average construction costs vary from $35 to $600 per acre, depending on local prices and conditions.

Farmers in southeast Asia, where shrimp farming is done on a comparatively large scale, drain their nursery ponds before stocking them with shrimp fry. They let the sun dry the bottom, then fill it with a few inches of water that has been thoroughly screened to avoid the entrance of unwanted organisms. The shallow water soon heats and small plants and animals that live on the bottom begin to thrive. These are a major source of food for shrimp and are left to grow until they become abundant, when the level of the water is raised to about a foot, and the small seed shrimp are placed in the pond. After the seed shrimp have reached juvenile size they are taken from the nursery ponds and placed in a rearing pond that

Feeding shrimp in ponds. *Courtesy of Louisiana Wild Life and Fisheries Commission, Marine Laboratory*

is much larger. Prior to this, the rearing pond has been emptied, dried, and then filled with screened water to a depth of three or four feet.

In Formosa and in the Philippines the procedure is similar. Seed shrimp are gathered by stretching bunches of living water plants across shallow bays or in salt water creeks. Young shrimp that migrate to these areas cluster around the plants, making it easy for collectors with nets to bring them in. The fry are placed in containers made of thick earthenware and taken to nurseries. Sometimes the shrimp are caught by opening the pond's sluice gates to incoming tides, and screening the water as it recedes, thereby trapping the thousands of baby shrimp that have come in with the tide. The one drawback to this method is that many other organisms are also caught, some of which may be undesirable.

Harvesting shrimp from ponds. *Courtesy of Louisiana Wild Life and Fisheries Commission, Marine Laboratory*

Harvesting shrimp in the Asian countries is usually done by one of three methods: (1) the pond is drained and the shrimp are picked up by hand; (2) a bamboo screen shrimp trap is used that sometimes has lights to attract them. It sends the crustaceans along a leader to the heart of the trap where they are bunched together and netted easily; (3) a bag net is placed at a sluice gate and, as the water flows through, the shrimp are caught in the net.

A trial program has been started in the United States for rearing shrimp in large tanks containing shallow water. Nutrients are added to the sea water so that plankton can grow, and these are used as shrimp food. Shrimp have also been raised in aquaria, but neither method has been successful enough to provide good stocks of seed shrimp for farmers.

In 1969 the first commercial shrimp farm in the state of Florida was in full operation on a five-acre site at St. Andrews Bay. This was the first attempt, outside of Japan, to breed, hatch, grow and market shrimp commercially. In tests conducted earlier on the farm results showed an increase of 1000% over natural conditions in the production of baby shrimp.

BAIT SHRIMP

In 1964 the regular bait shrimp industry in Texas and Florida alone was more than a two million dollar business. Sport fishermen like the small shrimp, live and dead, for bait when they go after game fish. Three kinds are use as bait: pink, white, and brown. These are caught at the juvenile stage after they leave the marshes and estuaries, a stage more desirable for bait than the larger adults that are used for food.

Otter trawls or shrimp boats supplied with nets make the catch in the bays close to the outlets. The catch is placed in a live well on board the boat, and then the shrimp are sorted. Trash fish are thrown back. If blue crabs are found they are sold later for bait. Dead shrimp are kept to be sold to the dead bait market. Live shrimp are either kept in a well with fresh sea water or placed in barges towed behind the shrimp trawler.

In port, the live shrimp are either sold immediately or are put in holding pens to await a higher market price. One type of pen is a large box placed in the water at the dock, in which the shrimp are kept alive by the natural tides and currents flowing through screened openings in the box. Another type of pen is a concrete watertight tank situated on land, with sea water pumped in at regular intervals.

Measuring shrimp in the laboratory. *Courtesy of Robert K. Brigham, Bureau of Commercial Fisheries, U.S. Fish and Wildlife Service*

Shrimp are priced in the U.S. at so much a dozen, about fifty to ninety cents, or sold to retailers directly from the boats for twelve to fifteen dollars a thousand.

Food shrimp are usually netted further out, near spawning grounds such as those located well off the Florida coast. A ten-foot net is thrown over the side to locate a shrimp school. After a school has been found the main trawl is used — a net 120 feet wide at the mouth. On occasions two boats work together, pulling a single large net between them. White shrimp are sought during the day. Brown and pink shrimp hide in the sandy bottom during daylight hours, so these must be fished for at night.

6

Oyster Culture

A young lawyer recently walked into a Maryland restaurant where he ordered a drink and a half dozen raw oysters. He ate the oysters and finished his drink but, upon receiving the check, discovered he had left his wallet in the office. He asked if he could pay later but the barman, after observing that the lawyer was six feet tall and weighed about 300 pounds, offered him a deal: if he would eat all the oysters he could possibly hold he would not have to pay the bill. The object was to set a new world's record for eating raw oysters. The lawyer patted his belly, wrapped a napkin around his neck, and ate and ate and ate. When he finally had to call it quits he had stuffed in more than 400 raw oysters. While it was not a world record it did promote endless publicity for the Maryland restaurant and its fine oysters. The world's record had been set by Joe Garcia of Melbourne, Australia in 1955 — 480 oysters eaten in just 60 seconds!

The state of Maryland is known as the number one producer of oysters in all the United States. Oyster harvesting throughout the east coast region has dropped drastically in the last half century and Maryland has won its position through developing leadership in a process called oyster culture, which takes various forms.

Before oyster culture is discussed it might be helpful to tell more about the oyster itself. As a food, oysters are eaten raw, in oyster stew, or cooked in various other ways. The oyster is popular throughout the world. Examples are the French oyster, the English Whitstables, the Blue Points from Long Island, N.Y., the Chincoteagues and the Chesapeake Bays. It has often been stated that oysters are only good to eat during the months that have an "r" in them but the real truth is that the months without an "r" — May, June, July and August — are the months when the oysters spawn, and common sense dictates that during these months they should be left free to increase their population. In some areas of the United States it is requested that anyone collecting oysters from certain areas return shells to the bays when the meat has been removed. This is done because baby oysters that have just been spawned swim around for some time before settling down in one place for the remainder of their lives, and oyster shells make a fine resting place for these tiny oysters. For this reason it is the law in Florida that the shells belong to the state after the oysters have been shucked, if they were taken from public grounds.

A female oyster will release 15 to 100 million eggs in one spawning. In a few hours the eggs become free-swimming larvae, called veligers, which drift around with the currents for two or three weeks until they attach themselves, with a little foot, to a clean surface. Once attached, they begin to form their shell. This is the spat stage, a name that comes from the old idea that the female oyster spat out her eggs. As they grow, the oysters take in food by pumping water between their two shells, called valves. Tiny organisms are caught by hair-like

Commercial oyster farm in Oyster Bay, Long Island. *Courtesy of Robert K. Brigham, Bureau of Commercial Fisheries, U.S. Fish and Wildlife Service*

stalks that surround the gills. As the food is caught it is passed along to the mouth by the hairs.

Using his knowledge of this development, the marine scientist has been able to make good progress in oyster culture in the United States. Oyster farming is not a dream of the future as it is with lobsters and most fish. It is already done on a much larger scale than shrimp farming. In the state of Massachusetts the natural haul has slipped 83.3% in the last 50 years and it has declined in other states. This has prompted men in Florida, Maryland, California and elsewhere to study the situation. They find that the tidal areas of estuaries are best for farming oysters as well as shrimp and fish. While fish can be kept in one pond until maturity and shrimp may be moved only once or twice, oysters must be moved often to many locations during their early stages of life.

It takes about four to five years for an oyster to grow in natural ways until it is of a size to be eaten raw on the half shell. This period can be cut in half with proper farming. One common method begins with choosing mature adult oysters selected according to growth, shape and size. These oysters are put in a tank and kept at a temperature of 50°F for a short period. The temperature is raised slowly to 65° where it remains for two weeks to a month, depending on the season of the year. The temperature is next raised to about 77° at which time spawning begins and the fertilized eggs are released. The eggs are placed in rearing tanks where the water is drained every two days. The large larvae that are capable of rapid growth, about 20% of the total, are caught in a fine mesh screen and placed in another tank that has specially prepared water. The water is cleared of animals so that only the smaller algae on which the tiny oysters feed are allowed to grow. If not enough algae are present more are added. Algae are grown in purified and enriched sea water in rooms that are kept at constant warm temperatures. It is important that at least two different kinds of algae be used as food for the oyster larvae, since one kind is not sufficient for a proper diet. When the oyster is young a daily ration of algae is usually 4,000 to 6,000 single-cell plants per oyster. As the larvae grow, the number of the algae used is increased.

After about two weeks the tiny oysters are ready to be set. They are placed in large plastic settling tanks capable of holding 800 gallons of water and 10 bushels of oyster shells carefully scrubbed to prevent bacterial growth. The shells cover the bottom of the tank where the larvae settle. One or two days are needed to complete the attachment. Once the spat is set, the shells are placed in netlike bags and are hung from beams over the nursery tank. They are fed more algae poured into these 6,000 gallon containers from storage tanks on the roof. The growth of the oysters is rapid during the week or so they are kept in this seaside greenhouse. After the week is up they are taken, still in the bags, to a dock and hung on floating rafts in a pond. Each raft holds 200 bags. The little seed oysters remain here for about three weeks until they grow to a half inch across, at which point they are large enough to be planted in oyster beds. This whole operation takes between four and six weeks.

The one danger to the above method is that very cold water can kill the oysters while they are hanging from the rafts in the pond or bay. Just as the lobster farmers are working with the power companies, the oyster farmers may learn to do the same and heat the water in the bay during the winter months so that oyster growing may be extended to a year-round operation. This should work because warm water from power plants seems to be non-toxic to shellfish and tends to support a tremendous growth of algae. But whether this thermal pollution harms other life has not been determined.

With the growing period extended to include the whole year it may be possible to grow oysters to adult size while reducing the growing time by a year or even two. This would make oyster farming a profitable venture. As new nuclear power plants are constructed for other coastal towns it may become possible to build them in conjunction with other seafood farms.

There are three main causes for the loss of oysters. First, silt can build up until it covers the small, first-year oysters, interfering with their growth and feeding, and possibly smothering them. Second, predators such as the oyster drill are very destructive, wiping out whole beds

Oysters hanging from rafts. *Courtesy of Department of Fish and Game of California, Menlo Park, California*

in a short time. The drill can be removed by cleaning the oyster beds with Polystream, a substance that has proven to be very effective. The starfish, another predator, is held in check by sprinkling quicklime on the beds at dead low tide during a period of calm. The dose is one ton per acre, about the same as the Polystream. Since starfish are always on the move, the farmer must constantly check to make sure this sea animal does not return to the pond. Third, MSX, an oyster disease, can cause considerable damage to populations, but scientists have found that seed oysters have fairly good resistance to it.

Interesting work is being done now on oyster farms like a small one in Orleans on Cape Cod. Clean oyster shells are placed on nylon strings and lowered into a vat containing spat. After the spat has cemented itself to the string of shells, they are taken outside and tied to rafts. The rafts are then towed to the center of a salt water pond that has previously been cleaned of debris and predators, and the bottom covered with shells or gravel. As many as 3,000 strings can be set out in this manner on one raft complex.

Developing a hatchery requires an expenditure of between $100,000 and $200,000, a staff of three people, and a half-dozen laborers. On a year-round scale, one half billion seed oysters could be produced each year by such a hatchery — enough to supply the requirements for seed oysters in the United States without importing any from Japan. These seeds could be ready for market in about two years when they are three or four inches in length.

White spots on the scallop shells are small oysters that have set while the shells were suspended in the water, one method of producing oyster seed. *Courtesy of State of Maine: Department of Sea and Shore Fisheries*

Robert M. Ingle of the Florida Board of Conservation has experimented in the feeding of artificially kept oysters as compared with those in natural surroundings. Many foods were tried in the laboratory such as microscopic live plants, powdered milk, and corn starch, but none of these worked well enough to fatten the oysters. Next, corn meal was ground to a very fine powder and placed so it would drift in the experimental tanks. The oysters immediately opened up their shells and kept them open, feeding constantly. During these studies it was found that the oyster accumulated food reserves and grew larger around the shell edges.

The Ingle investigators then studied the importance of currents to the growth of oysters, since these bivalves are found in both active and calm water. The oyster does not move around during its life, so food must come to it by the action of the currents. The oyster can only help itself in feeding by moving microscopic hairs located near its mouth. This causes very little motion and it is believed by marine biologists to be of scant assistance.

In one field experiment the Ingle staff examined an oyster reef off the coast of Florida and found that the oysters living on the reef were so small that they might be of another species. But, indeed, they were the same American oyster so dearly loved by connoisseurs of seafood. How did this happen? These oysters only grew to a very small size before dying and leaving their shells behind. A new generation would come along, attach to the older shells and build the reef a little higher. This continued until this twelve-mile reef near Cedar Key was peeking out of the water at low tide. As the years passed, the reef had risen so that it was out of water except at high tide. Being above water, these oysters were unable to feed except at high tide and the result was increasingly stunted oysters.

Oyster shells are picked up from Florida shucking houses to be dumped at sea to form oyster reefs. *Courtesy of Marine Research Laboratory, Florida Board of Conservation*

The Ingle group dug out a part of the reef with a huge crane attached to a floating barge. Oysters from the reef were transplanted into the dug-out areas. The currents were now able to flow through the reef one way and then the other according to the rise and fall of the tide. In two months the transplanted oysters were examined and found to have grown in size and improved in condition. Further studies are needed to determine what food can be used with these oysters that will be economical as well as effective.

It seems fair to assume that seed oysters, if they are placed where there is any kind of current bringing in natural food, will increase their growth.

Since 1949, Florida conservationists have been helping the natural oyster by building artificial reefs of oyster shells. The shells are picked up from the shucking houses and taken by truck to steel barges that tow them to areas off the coast. The shells are dumped in mounds to form an artificial reef. Mounds are considered the best way to eliminate the danger of new oysters being lost in silt and mud. It is believed these reefs will last for many years.

There are two main kinds of edible oysters, the cuplike, found off the Atlantic coast of the United States, in Europe, Canada, and in the Gulf of Mexico, and the flat oyster that is also collected in Europe and along the western coast of the United States where it is known as the Olympia oyster.

An oyster drag is used in harvesting the Olympia. An oyster barge floats over the grounds as the drag is pulled along the bottom. When the drag is full, its con-

Oyster shells being taken to sea by barge. *Courtesy of Marine*

tents are dumped on deck. Any oysters missed by the drag are picked up by hand during low tide, so that the bed may be cleaned and reseeded. Once the meats are taken out of the shells they are washed by jets of air and water to remove sand. As yet there is no fool-proof method of opening oysters other than by hand. It takes a skilled person to open the Olympia rapidly, but speed is essential since it takes 2,000 to 3,000 oyster meats to make a gallon. The meats are next dumped onto a grading table where they are selected for size and then packed into containers. The containers are sealed, placed under refrigeration and sent immediately to market where the oysters are sold as soon as possible since they lose their flavor very quickly.

Besides being useful as food, oysters are valued for their cultured and natural pearls. There are two species of pearl oyster: The Japanese and the Margarita pearl oyster found in Venezuela.

Research Laboratory, Florida Board of Conservation

Chesapeake Bay oyster dredge boat. *Courtesy of Robert K. Brigham,*

Bureau of Commercial Fisheries, U.S. Fish and Wildlife Service

In Japan near the sea village of Toba there is a large cultural pearl industry. Its pearl island is located a few hundred yards off shore. Pearl diving girls, called *amas,* dive to a depth of over thirty feet to harvest the oysters. The amas wear white cotton diving uniforms and are taken to the oyster grounds in small rowboats. They dive to the bottom, staying below for many minutes while harvesting. On surfacing, they drop the oysters into floating wooden tubs. Once on shore the oysters are pried open and their pearls are removed, cleaned, graded and sorted. When a necklace is to be made the pearls are first matched with others, then a hole is drilled in each and they are strung together.

To help the oyster make the pearl, a nucleus, or center that acts as an irritant, is placed in the oyster. The oyster reacts by surrounding the irritant with a secretion that forms the pearl. The Japanese have found the ideal irritant. Strangely enough, it is a piece of ground clam shell that comes from the Mississippi River.

Marine scientists have made it known that oyster farming does work and that there is enough acreage along U.S. coasts to provide sufficient oyster grounds. In fact, if only a fraction of the acres available were used it would quadruple the oyster production in the United States. However, this might bring the price down and the profits would decline. Nevertheless, oyster farming has been under way for many years and progress has been made. The day may come in the future when it will be as usual to see oyster farms and farmers as it now is to see cattle farms and cow hands.

7

The Soft Clam and Mussel Farmers

On any warm summer evening by the seacoast one gourmet delight is an old-fashioned clambake. The bake-master begins preparations early in the morning by digging a hole in the sand, placing beach stones inside and then building his fire. As the stones heat he takes potatoes, corn on the cob, lobsters, bread, sausages and frankfurters and wraps them in seaweed or foil and places them against the hot stones. He also takes buckets of soft-shelled clams, wraps them in foil or cheesecloth and puts them close to the fire. After everything has been slowly baked and gobs of butter melted, the bake-master begins serving the steaming clams. This is a favorite dish with a taste unlike anything else that is culled from the sea.

The clams used for steaming are sometimes called long necks or steamers. They are found on the west coast from California to Alaska, and from Labrador to North Carolina along the east coast. They are the main ingredient of clam chowder — New England style made with milk, or Manhattan style made with tomatoes. Fried clams are another favorite dish.

There is no doubt about the popularity of the soft-shelled clam, but can it be farmed with profit and success? The answer is no — at least not on the same basis as oyster farming because the demand is not as great and the price is lower. But clams are still suitable for farming and some work in this area has already been done by marine scientists and farmers.

The Japanese lead the way when it comes to clam culture. They raise clams in bays, harbors or tidal marshes. In some instances Japanese farmers transplant clams to less crowded areas. In others, they make sure the bottom is prepared so that young clams may be sown evenly and predators eliminated. For example, an area will be fenced off and the bottom prepared by using about 75 percent sand and 25 percent gravel and shells. In one experimental harvest sixty gallons of clams were dug from 36 square feet of bottom.

The soft-shelled clam is able to withstand wide changes in the salt content and temperature of the water. This is known since it has been dug both in the ocean where there is high salinity, and around estuaries where the salinity is low. Most commercial diggers work at low tide with a short-handled clam rake and a bucket. It is slow, hard work and the production of each man is limited, especially when cold or bad weather cuts into his working day.

Clams can also be harvested by using a hydraulic dredge attached to the side of a fishing vessel. This is towed with the front of the dredge touching the bottom and the rear angled upward toward the boat. A hose attached to the front shoots a high-powered stream of water into the muck, washing most of it away and leaving behind large pieces of sediment, rocks and clams. All this is taken by a conveyor belt toward the surface. The coarser sediments and small rocks fall through the conveyor while

Clam dredge. *Courtesy of Robert K. Brigham, Bureau of Commercial Fisheries, U.S. Fish and Wildlife Service*

Hard clam holding bed. *Author's photograph*

the stones, clams, and debris that remain are sorted by workers on the deck of the collecting vessel. One advantage of the dredge is that it permits deep water clamming, an area almost untouched by commercial fishermen of the past.

Like the oyster, the soft-shelled clam feeds on plankton or small plants and animals that float in the water. The clam moves very slowly and is only able to burrow into the mud or sandy bottom. It often stays in the same tiny area for months, and never gets far from where it started as a baby clam. Understandably then, it survives better where there is some sort of current that can bring food to its siphon and take the silt away. In stagnant water the clam can be suffocated by silt clogging its siphon.

The hard clam (quahog or little neck), the soft clam and the mussel have life histories that are similar. The females release eggs in the water. After hatching, the young are able to swim a little in a corkscrew motion, around and around, never really getting anywhere. But, moved by the currents and tides, the baby clams are soon swept away from where they were born. This is a good thing, for if the young clams were not carried away, the grounds around the adult clams would soon be overcrowded. Lack of space, food, and oxygen, would eventually destroy the clam beds.

After a week or two, the free-swimming young clam loses the tiny hairs it has used for propulsion and drifts to the bottom to remain for the rest of its natural life. It develops a strong muscle, or foot, at its lower end and gills and siphons begin to take shape. Since it is so small — about the size of a pin head — it attaches to grains of sand to keep from being swept away. A tuft of strong threads called a *byssus* are used by the clam for this purpose. Sometimes the threads are detached and the foot is used to move the clam, after which new threads are secreted.

Hard clams stored in sunken live cars in an estuary. *Author's photograph*

When the clam reaches a quarter inch in length it begins to burrow into the soft mud or sand, often making several attempts before it finds just the right spot. The threads are used to hold it fast at first, but then they disappear. Here the clam stays, maybe for as long as twenty-five years, if it is not found and eaten. Some grow to be five or more inches in length.

The hard clam is eaten on the half shell like an oyster and is called the little neck or cherrystone. These are usually about two or two and a half inches in length and make a tasty first-course dish. The hard clam is found along the east coast of the United States from Florida to Maine, with the greater abundance from New England to Virginia where living conditions are better. The very large clams, called bulls or coconuts, are dredged in deep water.

Aerating hard clam bed. *Author's photograph*

The hard clam is farmed to a much greater extent than the soft clam in the United States. In Florida, at Alligator Harbor, a method of farming the hard clam was tested. Pens were set up in sand and mud, about 100 feet from the low water mark, and enclosed by fences six feet high. The fences were set deep into the mud to keep out burrowing predators. Ten to 75 clams per square foot were seeded in the mud. Unprotected plots were also planted to be used as control areas for comparison. Each month samples were taken from both the protected and unprotected plots. The clams were measured and the number of dead counted. The results showed that the protected clams grew more than a millimeter a month, except those in the heaviest populations. In the unprotected plots all the clams were dead within a short period of time. Out of a total of 25,000 clams planted in the plots 18,000 survived and were eventually sold. The death rate in the fenced pens was a little above 25% as against the 100% rate of the unprotected clams. Examination of the shells of the unprotected clams showed cracks in most cases, evidence that the blue crab and the lightning welk were the predators responsible for the damage. The experiment also revealed that a thick layer of mud accumulated within the pens. This was attributed to the fact that the fences slowed the circulation of water. Few of the clams died because of this mud but it is known that siphon animals can suffer from too much silt as was accidentally demonstrated earlier in the experiment when a boat basin was dredged nearby, sending silt eight inches deep into some of the pens. In these pens all the clams were killed where the silt was deepest, and about half died where the silt was four inches thick.

Studies have been made along the Georgia coast by the Marine Fisheries Division of the Georgia Game and Fish Commission. In sample diggings in 432 intertidal stations, hard-shelled clams were found in only 41 of the areas, or in less than 10% of the samplings. Clams were then brought in from a hatchery in North Carolina to see if these same estuaries could sustain protected clams. The results were interesting: unprotected beds were soon wiped out by the blue crab while protected beds showed such good growth that it was estimated the clams would reach market size in just one year. These results were almost identical to those of the previous experiment noted earlier in Florida.

The trials demonstrated that clams can be farmed, if they are not planted too closely at the start and are protected from predators.

Mussel culture might become a large farming venture of the future except for the problem of demand. In the United States it is easy to sell clams, oysters, lobsters and shrimp because they are considered delicacies and the public wants them. And, as mentioned earlier, what is in demand brings a good price so that it pays to be a supplier. But the mussel has not yet hit it off in the mind of the United States consumer. The mussel is similar to the oyster and the clam, living on the organisms that it siphons in from the sea. It is, therefore, a prime animal for farming since it does not require that the farmer supply a great amount of food. One unusual fact about the mussel is its value as a food. Mussel meat has a high nutritional value averaging about 13% protein, 8% glycogen and 2.4% fat. Clams and oysters, on the other hand, have between 1% and 5% protein, and 2% glycogen aid 0.1 to 0.6% fat.

In the western parts of Spain, Holland, France and Italy mussels are raised in great quantities. Farming is done by two methods. One method, bottom raising, starts when the farmer buys seeds that have been dredged and plants them on the bottom of a pond already prepared in a fashion similar to the oyster ponds. At the time of planting each baby mussel is about a half inch in length. Within a year the mussel has grown an additional inch, and within three years it reaches two and a half inches in length and is ready to market. Sometimes a farmer will bunch some mussels together even though he knows they will remain half-sized due to overcrowding. This is done so that if the farmer needs more mussels after harvesting or has extra space he can thin out these clusters and have another full crop.

The starfish readily attacks these dark-shelled animals as it does the oyster. Large numbers of starfish can wipe out whole beds of mussels in a short time. When the enemy has advanced into the bed the farmer will dredge up both the mussels and the starfish. Out of the water starfish soon die while the mussels are able to live for many hours and do not mind the surface stay. Sprinkling salt over the dredged animals will speed the death of the predators. After the starfish are dead, the mussels are returned to the bed to continue their growth. If ready for harvesting the mussels are placed in an area without sand where they will, in time, rid themselves of any coarse sediments. After harvesting, they are taken to sheds where they are separated, washed and packed for market.

The second method is to grow mussels while they are hanging. This is more expensive since it takes more work and space to raise a crop. Poles are imbedded in the bottom and seed mussels attach to the outside of the poles. After the mussels are an inch long they are taken off the first poles and put into a netting hung between other poles. They stay this way for two years until they are ready for harvesting. Along the west coast of France there are about 300 miles of mussel-growing poles, with an annual yield of about 25 million pounds. Mussels are also

Mussels washed up on beach as a result of a winter storm. *Courtesy of Robert K. Brigham, Bureau of Commercial Fisheries, U.S. Fish and Wildlife Service*

grown on ropes hanging from frames built out over the water. In some areas the ropes are suspended from rafts. This method has had good results, with some mussels ready for market within a year.

The future of the shellfish industry will depend on the farmers of the 'sea. Oysters, lobsters, shrimp, and clams are becoming more and more popular in this country. A way is needed to preserve and provide an ample supply of these animals, which is not easy to do. It is important that a good location be chosen for the farms, one free of pollution and with proper temperature and salinity. There should be hatcheries to make seed available, and an abundance of plankton to be used as food.

The marine scientists of the future will experiment with genetics inside the hatcheries. Spawners will be selected for rapid growth, good shell shape, fatness of meat appealing colors and flavor. The spawners that adapt best to different areas will be kept, since sea farmers will be located all along the coastline where temperature, salinity and chemicals in the water will vary. It may become advantageous, for example, to grow seed clams in Maryland and fly them by air freight to Florida where, in the warmer water, the clams may be able to reach harvesting size within a year. Or eggs may be hatched in warm climates and sent north for growth. The location of the hatchery is not as important as where the shellfish are finally raised.

It will be essential in the future to learn to grow many different kinds of foods for the sea animals that will be high in nutrition and low in cost and maintenance. These foods will be available to the various types of shellfish and can be adapted for the different stages of development. In this way, super growth can take place, cutting cost and time. Special foods can also be used to produce certain flavors and colors in shellfish, thereby increasing their desirability and their market price.

New ways to cut down on predators are needed. A single crab entering a fenced farm can destroy thousands of seed clams in a few days. Fish and birds are dangerous, as are boring sea animals. All these must be kept out of the farming areas. A method often recommended to eliminate predators is using chemicals. This will require study since the use of chemicals near food alerts both scientists and the federal government. They require proof there will be no side or aftereffects from the chemicals.

Many types of shellfish can grow in partially polluted waters and are edible if they can be purified prior to consumption. Often they are dug up and replanted in clean areas and allowed to wash themselves pure in a year's time. A more rapid means of purifying is desirable and work on this has begun in Japan, England and the United States.

The entire farming system, from seeding to harvesting, needs to be more mechanized as too much of the work is still being done by hand. Eventually farming will be faster and there will be better shellfish for all.

Green turtle. *Courtesy of Miami Seaquarium*

8

Turtle Ranching

One of the most valuable reptiles in the world today is the green turtle. The price on its head grows higher and higher, but it was not always this way. At one time turtles were in great abundance. These reptiles go back to the Triassic period, about 200 million years ago, and man has been eating them throughout history. Broken turtle shells have been found among the very early remains of the Australopithecines in South Africa who lived more than 600,000 years ago.

Explorers of the early world sailed to the Caribbean and saw green turtles there in great numbers. They used them as a source of fresh meat, since by then the supplies aboard ship were usually exhausted. The turtles were snared and taken aboard alive where they were stored upside down on their backs until time to eat them. This may seem to be a heartless way to keep an animal, but herpetologists (who study reptiles,) claim it is easier for turtles to breathe out of water in this position. The bridges of the shell are weak and hinder breathing when the turtle is out of water and right side up. These bridges are supports located between the upper and lower shells and on land they do not hold up under the weight of the top shell.

Today, the green turtle is in great demand for many reasons. Turtle soup is made from a cartilage, known as the calipee, filling the spaces between the bones of the bottom shell. This is cut out from the adult turtle with a knife. Turtle eggs are eaten by man as well as turtle steaks. Turtle hides are used for leather and young turtles are stuffed and sold in shops for gifts. Hence the green turtle is a favorite prey of human predators as well as of its natural enemies.

From July to November the green turtles migrate from the open sea back to where they were born. It has not been determined how many years it takes for a turtle to reach maturity but at this time both males and females return to their native beaches where they mate offshore. After mating, the female heads for the beach. She pulls her many pounds of weight across the sand with her flippers until she reaches the upper edge, perhaps searching for the protection of a fallen tree or the base of a dune. Here she clears away the sand with her front flippers to make a resting area, and digs a nest with her flippers in the sand where she will deposit about 100 eggs. She then covers the nest, spreading the sand to disguise her laying area, and returns to the sea. She remains offshore about 13 days before coming ashore again to lay more eggs. She does this between three and seven times, each time digging a new nest. When her last eggs are laid she goes back to the deep sea, from which she will not return for another two or three years.

About two months later the leathery-skinned eggs, about the size of golf balls, begin to split open in the warm sand. Baby green turtles, about two inches in length, struggle to crawl out. They fight their way up through

the sand and eventually reach the surface to start immediately on a most dangerous journey to the sea. Birds seem
to know when the eggs have opened and hover overhead,
waiting. They swoop down, pick up the tiny turtles, and
fly off with a tasty meal. The baby turtles that reach the
sea have to face yet more birds who dive under the water
for them. Many turtles that escape the birds are eaten
by ghost crabs or gulped down whole by large fish. When
the crabs attack by clawing out their eyes the infants lose
their ability to locate the sea. Some scientists say these
ghost crab attacks could be a valuable clue in learning
how the baby turtles know in what direction to go to find
the water. Dr. Nicholas Mrosovsky of the University of
Toronto believes the tiny green turtles have a directional
sense — that they head for the brightest horizon, which
would be the sea. The babies find the sea even though it
is far out of sight from the nest. In experiments, turtles
have been picked up and turned around or obstacles have
been put in their way, but they eventually move in the
direction of the sea again.

Little is known of the habits and wanderings of the
green turtle while it swims the vast ocean but it always
returns to its former nesting grounds after traveling thousands of sea miles during the two or three years between
breedings. The United States Navy has taken more than
a passing interest in this phenomenon as it indicates an
advanced stage of navigation that might help the Navy in
improving its own navigation.

It is known that the Atlantic green turtle feeds on
the west coast of Africa and along the east coasts of the
Central American countries in the Caribbean Sea. There
are also feeding grounds along the west coast of Florida
in the Gulf of Mexico. Nesting grounds are now mainly
in the Aves Islands in the West Indies, at Tortuguero in
Costa Rica, on Ascension Island, midway between Africa

and South America, and along the northeast coast of South America. Former nesting places like the Cayman Islands below Cuba, the Dry Tortugas below Florida and the Bermuda Islands are no longer used as breeding areas because of the massive destruction of turtles carried out by men in these places over the years.

Turtle feeding grounds consist of an underwater pasture thick with tall grasses called turtle grass. From Florida to Brazil, in the shallow waters of the tropics, these marine grasses grow from a few inches to sixty feet in height. These undersea plants are rich and make the green turtle a very edible animal — 40% lean meat, tasty and nourishing.

Because man has destroyed so much of the turtle population by taking the females while they were nesting — often even before they could deposit their eggs — and by killing the males offshore, it is feared that the turtle herds may never recover.

Dr. Archie Carr, zoologist at the University of Florida, has been working for years to help preserve turtles, especially the green. At Tortuguero Beach on the eastern shore of Costa Rica, Dr. Carr has established the Turtle Bogue hatchery. Here green turtles are raised for study and the hatchlings are flown by plane to 28 sample beaches when they are a few days old. The beaches selected are those that green turtles formerly used for nesting before man destroyed them. The idea is to see if these baby turtles will grow to adult size in the sea and then return at nesting time to the beach where they were released.

In the past ten years Dr. Carr and his crew have transplanted 100,000 eggs and airlifted an equal number of baby turtles to beaches. As the mother turtle releases her eggs, the crew digs them out of the sand and takes them to the beach hatchery. Here they are reburied in sand and enclosed in chicken wire cages to keep away predators such as crabs. The cages also make it easy to locate the nests later to see if there are any nests that remain unhatched. After two months the baby turtles emerge and immediately head for the side of the cage that is closest to the sea. They are collected, placed in wooden tanks, and fed chopped fish. Later they are transferred to cardboard boxes and taken by air to designated beaches for release. If this experiment proves successful it may launch a program for restocking the green turtle population.

Dr. Robert E. Schroeder, Vice-President of Mariculture Limited located in Grand Cayman Islands in the British West Indies is expected to release 20,000 10-pound yearling turtles during the next year. In about three years the turtles should reach 100 pounds and then they will be harvested.

According to Dr. Schroeder, even if these systems work, new regulations regarding the green turtle will have to be made and enforced. But it is difficult to patrol great lengths of beaches. Eventually each turtle rancher may have his own section of beach. There he can guard the nests while the eggs are in incubation and keep the babies for a few weeks until they can leave for the sea with a good chance for survival. While these turtles fatten and grow in the turtle grass another crop of turtles, bred at an earlier date, would return to mate. For the sake of conservation, only a stated number of the females would be killed for market and then only after they had nested. A restricted number of the males would also be taken from the water offshore.

In the distant future, turtle grass areas may be fenced and the turtles released inside these enclosures. In these undersea pastures the turtle diet might be supplemented with ground fish or other food that would speed their growth rate. Also, as is now done with turkeys and other farm animals, the breeding turtles could be selected for their speed of growth, egg production, flavor and size, thereby producing a super turtle!

In recent years a program of tagging has been started in order to study the migratory habits of adult turtles. By the summer of 1967 more than 4,000 turtles had been tagged on the beaches. Each tag offered a reward for its return to a certain address and a request for information concerning the location and time that the turtle was found. By the end of 1967 almost 200 tags, or about 5% of the total, had been returned, some from more than 1,000 miles away. This tagging experiment will help to determine which types of turtle travel and where they go. It may even provide some knowledge of the turtle's life span.

9

Plants and Animals Collected
But Not Farmed

It was a warm fall evening as the bartender drew off a glass of beer and handed it to the customer. The liquid had a foamy head and as the bubbles rose the beer was clear and gold in color. At the same time, a few doors away, the girl behind another counter put chocolate syrup, milk and a scoop of ice cream in a milk-shake container, churned it in the machine for a few seconds, poured it into a glass and served another customer.

Strangely enough, there is a similarity between the contents of those two drinks. Both have a common ingredient — usually called seaweed. Ocean plants come in many sizes, shapes and colors, but some are useful in the manufacture of many products. In the beer, for instance, there is a substance called carrageen (after the town of Carrageen in southeast Ireland) that is derived from a certain seaweed. Its source is Irish moss, which is collected at low tide off the rocks along the North Atlantic coast, particularly in Scituate, Mass. and in Portland and Rockland, Maine. Carrageen is also used in milk puddings, suspensions of cocoa and chocolate milk, pie fillings, low-calorie foods, tooth paste, hand lotion, hair shampoo, water-based paints, and frosting mixes. It is even used to coat the bottom surfaces of ships to reduce the drag of water!

Moss gatherers, in boots and waterproof aprons, work in rowboats or dories equipped with outboard motors. They use long-handled rakes to scrape the moss from the rocks and toss it into the dories. If the sky is hazy and the water rough, oil is sprinkled on the water surface to calm it down and cut the glare, allowing the mosser to see the bottom. When the dory is filled, the mosser returns to port to sell his daily haul. The usual price is around 2¢ a pound for wet moss, and a good mosser can rake in more than 1,500 pounds per tide.

The moss is dried and rinsed and left on clean sand or concrete drying beds until the sun has bleached it almost white. Finally, the bleached moss is baled and shipped to a finishing plant where it is ground into powder and packaged for various manufacturers.

Seaweed's contribution to the milk shake was a substance called algin, used also in manufacturing ice cream and chocolate syrup. Algin is obtained from kelp, a long-stemmed sea plant that grows to a length of 750 feet from the sea bottom and can grow at a rate of one and a half feet a day. Giant kelp is found mostly off the coast of California and is gathered by large kelp harvesters, or floating barges that have shearing mechanisms capable of cutting the kelp four feet below the surface. In order to preserve the kelp grounds, this work is done under rigid controls set up by the California Fish and Game Commission. They govern the length of the cuttings so that only mature beds are harvested.

The uses of algin are many. It has the ability to make ink more permanent, to thicken salad dressing and ice cream, to keep a head on a mug of beer, to suspend the

Seaweed harvester raking Irish sea moss. *Courtesy of Marine Colloids, Inc.*

small particles in paints and hand lotions. It is used in ceramic glazes, in aspirin-compound tablets, penicillin suspension, calamine lotion, and dozens of other products.

Agar, a third important product of seaweed, is found principally in the lower California coastal waters. It is collected during the warm months by skin divers using regulation diving suits and underwater breathing equipment. After harvesting, it is washed daily with fresh water and then dried on racks for one or two weeks until it is sun bleached. After bleaching, it is packed into 200-pound bales and shipped to the manufacturer. Agar is used in growing cultures in the field of bacteriology. It is utilized in gel form in both medicine and dentistry. In medicine it is used as a laxative, as an ingredient of health foods and as an emulsifier. Dentists use the substance for making teeth impressions. Meat canners use it for jellying chicken, fish and meat and in products where a non-animal stabilizer or gelatin is required, as in Kosher foods.

Seaweed may prove to be a benefit to mankind in still another way. A certain chemical in it may provide protection against radioactive fallout. This chemical, sodium alginate, can absorb strontium-90 in great quantities. Strontium-90 is dangerous because it may cause leukemia or bone cancer if taken into the system in excessive amounts. People who have eaten food containing strontium-90 could offset its effect by consuming sodium alginate also as this chemical will absorb the strontium while it is in the intestinal tract.

TURTLE GRASS

As mentioned earlier, turtle grass is an important sea plant. Off the coast of Florida, there are about four million acres of this grass, with a potential yield of 11 million

Unloading turtle grass. *Courtesy of Bureau of Commercial Fisheries, College Park, Md.*

tons of edible leaves. There are also vast areas of turtle grass in the southern portion of the Caribbean. It is a rapid grower — each leaf or blade lengthening about an inch in a week. The plants grow both horizontally and lengthwise, sending out runners. After a growth of about one or two feet, the leaves break off and the resulting leaf decay provides nutrients to support the teeming life of tiny sea animals such as worms, fishes, snails and plankton. A study has been undertaken to determine if this grass could be used, with commercial profit, as a foodstuff for land animals. In the first phase of the test, a collection of grass was washed and chemical samples taken. The results showed that reducing its salt content by washing for 15 minutes in fresh water increases the value of the grass since livestock are able to eat more of it.

In the second phase of the test, the grass was fed to sheep for a period of three weeks. The results indicated that it is not adequate as a complete diet, but is beneficial if added to alfalfa and corn.

Turtle grass has not yet been harvested in any great quantity but since it now can be used to supplement the diet of land animals all that may be needed is to develop an inexpensive means of harvestng it.

Drying turtle grass. *Courtesy of Bureau of Commercial Fisheries, College Park, Md.*

SEA URCHINS

A few years ago the valuable kelp grounds off the coast of California were in trouble. The sea urchin, a spiny little animal related to the sand dollar and starfish, had begun to feed on the kelp and soon had the beds all but stripped clean. Marine scientists were awarded a grant to study and remedy the situation, and soon discovered that quicklime was deadly to the sea urchin. Lime was dropped by plane over the kelp grounds. Within a week the sea urchins died and within three weeks the kelp had begun to grow back.

It is now hoped that the sea urchin might be promoted as a food delicacy. In the United States the reproductive organs of the sea urchin are eaten by enough people to have led to the building of a tiny sea urchin fishery off the coast of Maine. Since World War II the average yearly catch of urchins has been about 75,000 pounds, worth between $3000 and $4000 in the food market. If this sea animal became more popular as a food, it could be collected regularly for the market. Finger-nail sized orange segments of the gonads are served as a seafood cocktail and are said to be as tasty as oysters or cherrystone clams. Some say they are even tastier than caviar.

SQUID AND OCTOPUS

Other sea animals that are edible but not in much demand in the United States are squid, octopus and cuttlefish — all cephalopods. In Europe, Asia, and the islands of the Pacific these animals are eaten either fried or boiled or dried by the sun. In large U.S. cities with a sizeable foreign population, octopus and squid are sold in the fresh fish markets. They are netted by fishing boats and brought to port quickly, usually the same day. Squid make a fine bait for food fish such as flounder or striped bass, and biology classes find the large, simple nervous systems of the squid ideal for study. Public aquariums feed octopus or squid to their seals and whales, especially when they need variety in diet. Their ink sac is used as paint by artists because of its natural brown pigment called sepia. The cuttlebone of the cuttlefish serves as a component in dentifrices, as a source for the lime and salts needed by caged birds, or when ground into a fine powder, as an abrasive.

SURF CLAMS

Unlike the soft and hard-shelled clams mentioned in Chapter 7, the surf clam is one of the largest bivalve animals taken from the sea for food. It is found along the east coast of the United States from North Carolina to Maine and the largest surf-clam fishery operates off the coast of New Jersey. Between 40 and 50 million pounds of clam meats are landed each year. The clams are dredged from water up to 100 feet deep and some have been taken at a depth of 500 feet. During storms the clams are often ripped loose from their beds in the sand and washed up on the beaches. After one storm in Long Island, New York, it was estimated that five million clams were stacked up on each mile of beach.

About 60 clam boats make up the fleet that leaves the New Jersey coast each day five days a week. These boats are out for an average of 12 to 14 hours. On their return to port the clams are unloaded and hosed down

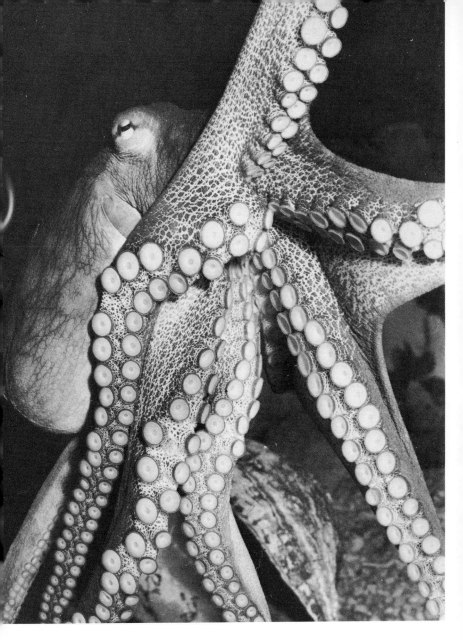

Octopus. *Courtesy of Miami Seaquarium*

before being stored in cold rooms. The next morning the clams are placed in fresh hot water for about a half minute so that the shells will open slightly, making them easier to shuck. The shucking is done by hand and then the meats are placed in a washer to remove bits of shell and sand. Finally, the meats are packed in large tanks and shipped off to be processed. They are used mainly in making clam chowder, clam cakes, and even clam juice.

CRABS

Crabs are caught at an average yearly rate of more than 250 million pounds at a value of about 30 million dollars, according to the United States Bureau of Commercial Fisheries. There are numerous methods for catching crabs that range all the way from a boy wading in the water with a net to dredging vessels that set out with a crew of four. The most marketable crabs are the rock crab, blue crab and king crab. These make up the greater part of the industry and bring the highest prices. The Dungeness crab, the stone crab, the red crab and the Jonah crab are less popular but still edible. In the last few years fresh and canned crab meat has become much in demand, with the king crab fast approaching the popularity of shrimp and lobster.

The king crab lives on the continental shelf off the coast of Alaska. It often measures five feet across and weighs up to 24 pounds. Mid-winter is the best season for catching it. Crabbing vessels carry about 30 traps, each trap being about the size of a twin bed. These traps are expensive; if one is lost with all its gear it can cost more than $1,000 to replace it. Each trap weighs between one and two thousand pounds and requires two men plus hydraulic gear to help haul it onto the deck. One man steadies the cable and the other operates the winch.

Frozen herring serves as bait. A big catch might have several eight to ten pound crabs in each trap, but the usual haul will be about 50 smaller crabs. To speed processing, the king crab is cooked for a short time to loosen the meat before pressure jets of water force it from the shell. The meat from the shoulder, leg and claw is all that is edible and the rest of the crab is tossed overboard. Once the meat has been cleaned it is packed into containers ready for canning.

The blue crab is caught and marketed in both its soft and hard-shelled stages. It is also a potential species to be farmed as mentioned in the next chapter. A soft-shelled crab is one that has outgrown its old hard shell, shucked it, and is left with a new one that is wrinkled and soft. Soft -shelled crabs are in greater demand than hard because the entire body can be eaten. Since blue crabs are much smaller than king crabs, the pots are only two feet square and the crabs enter through funnels that taper inward and make escape difficult. The blue crab is also caught with baited lines, trawls and dredges. In one method, a long length of baited line is laid on the bottom with each end anchored and buoys marking its location. After a short wait a fishing boat carefully hauls one end of the line up to the surface with the harvest of crabs still attached to the bait. As the line nears the fishing boat many crabs drop off but men with dip nets are poised ready to collect them.

SPONGES

The sponge is an interesting animal because it looks so much like a plant. It is a multicellular creature of the sea that has proved to be useful to man and is collected regularly. The valuable part is the skeleton — compressible, tough and capable of taking in large amounts of water. Some of the sponges collected off the coast of Florida can absorb 25 to 30 times their dry weight.

Divers in rubber suits descend to depths of 100 feet to find the sponges. They pick them off the bottom with a short-handled hook and place them in a mesh bag. When the bag is full the diver sends it to the surface and an empty bag is lowered along the life line. Each diver works two hours at a time and then is replaced by another. If the water is very deep the diving time must be reduced. After the sponges are gathered they are left on the deck to decay for about two days, then the tough outer skin is scraped away and the sponges are washed and dried. They are sometimes bleached to give them a better color but since this weakens the fibers it is done only with the darker sponges. Prices for sponges average seven to eight dollars a pound. When sponges became scarce after World War II, artificial sponges made of cellulose and plastic were introduced and these have gradually replaced the natural sponges.

SEALS

The Pribilof Islands off the coast of Alaska in the Aleutian chain are the breeding grounds for the fur seals that provide coats and other garments for the women of the United States and the world. In years past about 69,000 sealskins have been taken annually. It was not until the late 1700's, after an 18-year search, that the location of these breeding grounds was finally discovered. Wholesale slaughter of the seal began after this discovery. At that time the seal herd was estimated to be about two and a half million but men killed the seals for pelts and oil at such a rate that huge populations were wiped out south of the equator where only a few small herds can be found today.

By the year 1910 the herd on the Pribilof Islands had been reduced to less than 150,000 animals and a convention was called including delegates from the United States, USSR, Canada and Japan to draw up plans for limiting this destruction. Under careful controls that allow only the males to be killed, the present-day herd has increased to about one and a half million animals. Still larger herds are assured as long as the countries of the world continue to work together. At one time, after the seal had been skinned, the carcass was left to rot on the rocks. This was considered such a terrible waste of valuable meat and other products that a plant was built on the islands to produce oil and seal meal. The oil was used for tanning leather until recently when this market died out. Seal meal first served as fish feed in chicken hatcheries and later was sold as a protein supplement for poultry feeds. In the early 1960's a private firm began shipping frozen seal meat to mink breeding farms, and by 1965 more than a million and a half pounds of seal meat had been marketed in this manner.

Stone crab. *Courtesy of Wometco Miami Seaquarium*

10

Potential Plants and Animals to Farm

BLUE CRABS

In the United States the blue crab — already a popular seafood as mentioned earlier — may someday be farmed. Experiments have begun in Japan and scientists are waiting for the results.

The crab has a unique life cycle. In the fall, after the female has molted, breeding takes place and during the winter the sperm is stored within the female. In the spring, as the eggs are laid, the sperm is released, fertilizing the eggs, which remain on the outside of the female for about a month until they hatch into free swimming organisms. During the following four weeks there are several growth stages before the juvenile stage, when they stop swimming and settle to the bottom. There they stop eating plankton and begin to scavenge for other food such as dead fish.

In one blue-crab farming experiment, the egg bearing females are caught at sea and taken to the laboratory where they are placed in large tanks. Once the eggs are hatched the babies are fed tiny marine organisms for the first week and then brine shrimp for the remainder of the swimming period. At the juvenile stage, each tank may hold 30,000 tiny crabs feeding on fresh fish meat — usually anchovy, as this is inexpensive and available in large quantities. During the next 20 days, although the juvenile crabs are fattened, their number drops to about 6,000 since crabs are cannibals and eat their own kind. This remains a major problem in raising blue crabs as they seem to prefer their own species, even when other foods are available. Any time two large crabs are in the same enclosure one eats the other. Raising the crabs in separate compartments may be the answer — perhaps a house for crabs, suspended from a buoy.

After about a year, the surviving blue crabs reach a length of six inches, which is considered to be a marketable size. This is not too long a period for growing animals that have such a high market value.

ABALONE

Abalone is a large, edible snail, with a shell that sometimes has value as mother-of-pearl. When used for food, the large foot is cut off, sliced, and then pounded with a wooden mallet to soften it. It is relished in California and other warm water areas and sells for a high price. Some experts on seafood describe it as the best tasting meat of all the mollusks.

In the farming process small abalone are kept in tanks where they feed on diatoms at first, then algae. Green alga, called Ulva, is the favorite food of young adult snails. After about eight months the abalone are large enough to be stocked, or taken to natural areas and released in the hope that they will grow to a marketable size and can be collected and sold. So far, time and space have proved to be such major drawbacks in the farming of abalone that one cannot as yet expect a good return.

CONCHS

Another large snail is the conch (pronounced KONK) — sometimes called the queen conch. It is found in the Caribbean Sea and off the coasts of Florida in the Atlantic Ocean and Gulf of Mexico. It is larger than the abalone, sometimes reaching a weight of over six pounds. Conch meat is eaten fresh or sun dried. In the Bahamas more than a quarter million dollars in marketable conch are brought in annually by the fishermen.

Like the abalone, the female conch has many eggs. She may release up to 750,000 but, unlike the abalone, the conch eggs produce tiny little snails that do not go through stages of development as drifting or swimming larvae. These snails eat sea grass and algae and need about two years to reach their full size.

In order to farm the conch, it would be necessary to restrict them in pens, since they tend to move about as they search for algae to eat. The fences could also protect the conch from predators such as the loggerhead turtle, the spiny lobster, the hermit crab, the octopus, and about a dozen species of fishes that feed on young snails. There are no other major difficulties in farming this species. However, since the price of conch in the shell is at present less than 25 cents a pound, this would not now be a profitable venture.

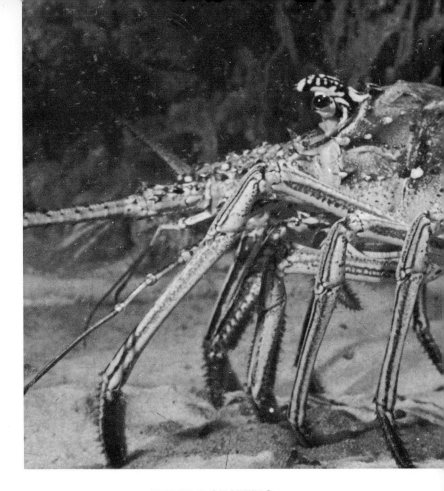

SPINY LOBSTERS

This sea animal is a relative of the more popular American lobster but it does not have the two large claws. It lives in warmer waters and is especially popular in Florida. It is also called crawdad, salt water crawfish or rock lobster. The eggs are carried on the outside of the female along the abdomen. When the eggs hatch, the lobsters, leaf-like in appearance, drift for three to six months. Those that survive this period settle to the bottom and look for rocky crevices in which to hide. They stay hidden

Spiny lobster. *Courtesy of Miami Seaquarium*

during the day and go out only at night to feed on clams, snails, and similar animals. While they are searching for food, predators such as jewfish, sharks, groupers and larger spiny lobsters are looking for them.

As yet, no satisfactory experiments have been made to determine the growth rate of the spiny lobster. This fact and the difficulties of the long drifting stage seem to make it economically unsound to farm this species until more research is done.

WORMS

The lugworm is located along all the coasts of the United States and makes fine bait for sports fishermen. There is great demand for bait as sports fishing has become a big business. The Sandy Hook Marine Laboratory of the United States Bureau of Sports Fisheries and Wildlife estimated that in 1965 eight million salt water fishermen caught 737 million fish weighing a total of one and a half billion pounds. The fish most often caught were bluefish, striped bass and flounder — all fish that can be caught with worms for bait.

Two of the most common bait worms are the blood worm and the clam worm. Diggers look for these at low tide along the North Atlantic coast. In 1966 more than one and a half million pounds of worms worth 1.3 million dollars at wholesale were dug in Massachusetts and New Hampshire.

Difficulties arise in attempting to raise either of these two popular worms. The clam and blood worms spawn in open water, and their young are spread in all directions by the currents and tides. The juvenile worms need a diet of plankton, which is hard for the farmer to produce or obtain.

The lugworm is better suited for raising than clam or blood worms since the eggs are not dispersed. The female lays her eggs in a burrow where they are encased in a jelly-like substance or capsule. After they are pushed out of the burrow they still remain anchored. The larvae develop within this substance and are released when they are of sufficient size to dig into the bottom sediment. Therefore, young lugworms can be collected by picking up their capsules from the bottom. While still inside the capsule the eggs do not need to be fed. Once they are released in the mud they feed on organic materials found in the sediment. They are rapid growers and do not suffer from overcrowding.

In one experiment, a plywood tray about three feet square and a foot high was filled with gravel and white sand after the bottom of the tray had been perforated and covered with a plastic screen to provide water circulation. The tray was set in a tank containing algae and a lugworm capsule was placed inside the tray. After six months the tray was raised and 72 lugworms were found, each about six inches in length. These were worth about three dollars on the market. The experiment showed that it is possible to raise lugworms but it has not yet been determined if it can be done economically on a large scale.

WESTERN RAZOR CLAMS

The razor clam of the west lives in the area from the Aleutian Islands southward to the beaches of southern California. It is a popular food item for chowder, especially in Oregon. It is estimated that about one and a half million razor clams are dug in Oregon each year, even though there is a legal limit set at twenty-four clams a day per family.

In the process of breeding, the eggs are released into the water where they will be fertilized if they chance to meet a sperm. Naturally, the mortality rate is high even though each female releases about six to ten million eggs a year. It takes between one and four months before the free swimming larvae settle to the bottom where they begin to make their shells. Even after the shells have set, about 95% of the clams die. Those that survive reach a harvestable size of three and a half inches in the first year.

Because of this short growth period they may be raised profitably. However, the young clams are susceptible to changes in salinity and water temperatures and may die if the environment is not suitable for them.

PLANKTON

It has long been known by marine scientists that plankton is a valuable food source for fish and other animals of the sea. We are only beginning to explore the possibilities of plankton as a food for man. If we are to have planktonburgers some day, then it will be necessary to discover a way to harvest or farm plankton.

Great quantities of plankton grow each year in the sea. Since the United States is a well-fed nation it has not yet been necessary to do research regarding the use of plankton as a food. During World War II the United States did make extensive studies to find out if plankton could be used as food by shipwrecked survivors and pilots shot down over the oceans. When it was found that this was possible, plankton nets became part of survival units.

Plankton collecting is a problem because there are few areas of sufficient concentration of these tiny animals and plants in the vast ocean. Tests have been made, however, in one area. In the estuaries and sea lochs off the west coast of Scotland 525 pounds of dry weight plankton were collected by using ten nets set out in the strong tides for a period of 12 hours — a period that allowed plankton to be collected from both the incoming and outgoing tides.

It is not known if there are any heavy concentrations of plankton along the coasts of the United States. There are some in the polar regions but adverse weather conditions would hinder collection, and the costs of transportation would be high. It has been suggested that these tiny creatures could be dried on factory ships, thereby reducing the bulk and the weight. Conservationists are concerned about the fact that heavy harvestings of plankton might take food from whales, clams, lobsters, fish, and other sea animals. However, marine scientists estimate that only about 10% of the whole ocean supply of plankton is actually used. If so, harvesting could be increased ten times, and plankton growth could be increased yet more by the use of fertilizers and cultivation.

Plankton might also be raised on shore in fully automated factories. This would make collection easy, transportation less costly, and would leave the ocean plankton for the sea animals.

Tiny plants like plankton can be raised in huge tanks when proper temperatures, lights, nutrients and water are available. The organisms are floated off from the tanks into containers. One such organism, an alga called Chlorella, grows very rapidly but experiments conducted in Japan, Europe, Israel and the United States have shown that growing this alga is expensive. Professor Hiroshi Tamiya of the Japan Tokugawa Institute found that Chlorella, under normal conditions, is composed of 50% protein, which contains all the amino acids needed for proper nutrition for man or animal. When grown in vats the algae must be stirred constantly in order to mix the carbon dioxide, and distribute the nutrients evenly. One method is to pump in air that has carbon dioxide. The gas is made by burning crude oil and mixing it with air before it is blown into the culture vats by a huge blower. Small parts of water and alga mixture are next taken off and placed in a centrifuge until a cake of alga is left. This is washed with water, dried, and ground into a fine green powder. If the process were carried on as part of a mass culture program it could produce 13 metric tons a year. This compares favorably in food value with 13 tons of sugar beet or six and a half tons of corn in fresh weight each year. In order to produce Chlorella economically a factory of about 100 acres in size would be needed and even then the cost of production could be over a dollar a pound. This could not compete on the market with MPC, soy beans, or alfalfa, any of which can be grown for under 15 cents a pound. However, this price does compare favorably with that of skim milk powder, which is about $1.20 a pound.

Undaria, a brown alga, has been cultured in Japan with more success. Fully mature plants are taken from the sea, brought into the laboratory and placed in plastic or concrete tanks. Inside the tanks are frames with cotton string hanging from them and the tiny zoospores released by the plants attach themselves to the strings. These are kept in cool and shady areas since the plants do not grow if the water becomes too warm. In the fall, when the ocean water is cool enough, the strings are transferred to the ocean where they are hung from long lines held by buoys, or from bamboo rafts. During the winter, harvesting is done either by removing the whole plant or by cutting off pieces of it. It is eaten by the Japanese either raw or dried, chopped into pieces, and served with raw fish or other seafood.

There is no doubt that man needs additional food, and that some part of this will come from the sea. How great that part will be is not yet known. Sea farmers are working every day to find out just what kinds of farming are practical, and what kinds will have to be abandoned. Any intensive system of rearing animals — whether they are sheep, chickens, oysters or fish — must depend on environment and scientific selection of the animals in order to insure that they will adapt to the conditions of culture. Predators must be kept out of the areas that are to be farmed. The feeding and breeding habits of the animals must be learned. Chemical nutrients must be kept in supply. This could be done by using the natural resources found among the deeper parts of the sea bottom. Through the upwelling that occurs naturally these nutrients reach the surface, and it may be possible to help mix these rich waters and increase the food available.

It is almost unanimously believed by marine scientists that the ocean can provide man with an enormous amount of additional food, and that the supply will stay ahead of the increase in population for a while. In order to achieve this, sea animals and sea plants that are not usually eaten will have to be used. There must be increased research in many fields of science, from the rudimentary study of the biology of plants and animals, to the problems involved in processing and marketing what is cultured and harvested. Ahead is a huge job for those men who will grow food in the largest pasture in the world — the sea.

GLOSSARY

cannibalistic — an animal that has a tendency to eat its own kind.

cholesterol — a fat-like substance found in eggs, oils and some meats.

estuary — the section of a river or stream that meets the sea. Here salt and fresh water mix. (*Estuarine* — pertaining to estuary.)

isotope — two or more forms of a chemical element that are alike except for the number of atomic particles in the nucleus.

marine protein concentrate — flour made from crabs, lobsters, shrimp or other marine animals

metabolism — physical and chemical processes that take place in the human body, resulting in available energy.

plankton — small plant or animal organisms, that passively float near the surface of the water.

quicklime — unslaked lime, a calcium compound.

radioisotopes — an isotope of an element, artificially made and designed to give off radiation so that it can be used in research.

salinity — the amount of salt in sea water or any solution.

sediment — small particles that settle to the bottom of a liquid.

zoospores — tiny spores produced by certain algae plants and some fungi. They move by means of flagells (long appendages that wave back and forth.)

BIBLIOGRAPHY

BOOKS

Bardach, John, Harvest of the Sea, New York: Harper & Row, 1968

Iversen, E. S., Farming the Edge of the Sea, London: Garden City Press, 1968

McKee, Alexander, Farming the Sea, New York: Crowell, 1969

Miller, Robert C., The Sea, New York: Random House, 1966

ARTICLES

National Geographic

Carr, Archie, Caribbean Green Turtle: Imperiled Gift of the Sea. June, 1967, pp. 876-890

Zahl, Paul A., How the Sun Gives Life to the Sea. Feb. 1961. pp. 199-225

Scientific American

Brett, J. R., The Swimming Energetics of Salmon. Aug. 1965, pp. 80-85

Hasler, Arthur D. and James A. Larsen, The Homing Salmon. Aug. 1955, pp. 72-76

Korringa, Pieter, Oysters. Nov. 1953, pp. 86-91

Milner, Harold W., Algae as Food. Oct. 1953, pp. 31-35

Riley, Gordon A., Food from the Sea. Oct. 1949, pp. 16-19

Sea Frontiers

Ashbrook, Frank G., The Beautiful Swimmer. Nov.-Dec. 1965, pp. 334-341

Bradfisch, Jean, Artificial Seaweed. Jan.-Feb. 1966, pp. 9-11

Havinga, B. H., Mussel Culture. July, 1964, pp. 155-161

Hillaby, John, The Fate of the Sea Turtles. Jan.-Feb. 1965, pp. 4-13

Ingle, Robert M., Artificial Food for Oysters. Sept.-Oct. 1967, pp. 296-303

Iversen, E. S., The King-Sized Crab. July-Aug. 1966, pp. 228-237

Schroeder, Robert E., Buffalo of the Sea, May-June 1966, pp. 176-183

Stephens, William, Ocean Harvest. May-June 1967, pp. 158-168

Stokes, George, Spiny Plague. Jan.-Feb. 1968, pp. 22-30

Williams, Hill, Breeding Superfish. Nov.-Dec. 1967, pp. 322-331

Oceanus

Ryther, J. H. and Matthiessen, G. C., Aquaculture, its Status and Potential, Feb. 1969, pp. 3-14

INDEX

36, 37; salmon, 30, 31, 32, 33; sardines, 27; striped bass, 33; supply, 18
Fish flour, 17, 18, 21; bisquits, 18
Fishing, lobster, 40
Fish reef, 35-36; material, 35; Gulf of Mexico, 36
Florida Board of Conservation, 62
Fremlin, J. H., 15
Fujinaga, Dr. Motosaku, 48

Garcia, Joe, 55
Grass, turtle, 86, 87, 92, 93, 94
Green Turtle, 83-87
Gulf of Mexico, 36

Hard-shell clam, 73, 75, 76
Hawaiian Islands, 30, 35
Herpetologists, 83
Histidine, 21
Hunting animals, 13

Infrared instruments, 22
Ingle, Robert M., 62
Iodine vapors, 22
Irish moss, 89, 90
Iselin, Columbus, 13
Isotope, radioactive, 22

Kaylor, Dr. John D., 22
Keating, Senator Kenneth B., 35
Keith, Representative Hastings, 36, 37
Kelley, John R., 33
Kelp, 90
Kilka, 22

Life, cycle, 11, 12; source, 11
Liquamen, 18
Lobster, boats, 40, 41; buoys, 40; catch, 41, 42; dragging, 41; eggs, 40; farming, 44, 45; fishing, 40, 41; limit, 42, 43;

location, 41, 42; molting, 40; pots, 40, 41; price, 39; raising, 42; spiny, 106, 107; young, 40
Long Island, N.Y., 34
Lugworm, 108, 109

Mackerel, 27
Mariculture Limited, 87
Marine protein concentrate, 16, 18-21, 33; processing system, 20
Milk, cow's, 21
Mink feed, 101
Mobile Bay, 33
Molting, lobster, 40
MPC, see Marine protein concentrate
Mrosovsky, Dr. Nicholas, 85
MSX, 60
Mullett, 30
Mussel, farming, 77, 78; hanging, 78; nutritional value, 77; poles, 78, 79; predators, 78

New Bedford, Mass., 19
Nuclear power plants, 44, 59

Octopus, 95, 96
Oils, fish, 21; unsaturated, 13
Oyster, as food, 56, 64; Cape Cod farm, 60; culture, 57; disease, 60; drag, 64; drill, 60; eggs, 56, 58; food, 62; growth, 58, 62; hatchery, 61; Ingle study, 62, 63; larvae, 58; losses, 59, 60; meats, 65; Olympia, 64, 65; pearl, 65-68; "R", 56; raft, 59; rearing tanks, 58; record eating, 55; reef, 63, 64; seed, 59, 63; settling tanks, 58; spat, 56, 59, 60; spawning, 56